Exploring Animal Rights

Series Editor: Cara Acred

Volume 233

Independence Educational Publishers

First published by Independence Educational Publishers

The Studio, High Green

Great Shelford

Cambridge CB22 5EG

England

© Independence 2012

Photocopy licence

The material in this book is protected by copyright. However, the
purchaser is free to make multiple copies of particular articles for instructional
purposes for immediate use within the purchasing institution.
Making copies of the entire book is not permitted.

British Library Cataloguing in Publication Data

Exploring animal rights. – (Issues ; v. 233)

1. Animal welfare – Moral and ethical aspects.

I. Series II. Acred, Cara.

179.3-dc23

ISBN-13: 9781 86168 626 8

Printed in Great Britain

MWL Print Group Ltd

Contents

Introduction

Exploring Animal Rights is Volume 233 in the **Issues** series. The aim of the series is to offer current, diverse information about important issues in our world, from a UK perspective.

ABOUT EXPLORING ANIMAL RIGHTS

Animal welfare relates to the general health and well-being of animals and covers a wide range of issues, from the care of family pets to concerns about exploitation, experimentation and abuse. How important is animal welfare? Do animals have rights too? If so, what are they? Is it ethical to use animals in medical research? This book explores these questions and more by investigating animal rights in the UK and globally.

OUR SOURCES

Titles in the **Issues** series are designed to function as educational resource books, providing a balanced overview of a specific subject.

The information in our books is comprised of facts, articles and opinions from many different sources, including:

- Newspaper reports and opinion pieces
- Website fact sheets
- Magazine and journal articles
- Statistics and surveys
- Government reports
- Literature from special interest groups

A NOTE ON CRITICAL EVALUATION

Because the information reprinted here is from a number of different sources, readers should bear in mind the origin of the text and whether the source is likely to have a particular bias when presenting information (or when conducting their research). It is hoped that, as you read about the many aspects of the issues explored in this book, you will critically evaluate the information presented.

It is important that you decide whether you are being presented with facts or opinions. Does the writer give a biased or unbiased report? If an opinion is being expressed, do you agree with the writer? Is there potential bias to the 'facts' or statistics behind an article?

ASSIGNMENTS

In the back of this book, you will find a selection of assignments designed to help you engage with the articles you have been reading and to explore your own opinions. Some tasks will take longer than others and there is a mixture of design, writing and research based activities that you can complete alone or in a group.

FURTHER RESEARCH

At the end of each article we have listed its source and a website that you can visit if you would like to conduct your own research. Please remember to critically evaluate any sources that you consult and consider whether the information you are viewing is accurate and unbiased.

What is animal welfare?

Animal welfare relates to the general health and well-being of animals and covers a wide range of issues, from the care of family pets to concerns about exploitation and abuse.

Animal rights are hotly debated. Proponents stress the helplessness and vulnerability of animals and campaign for their protection, particularly in areas such as medical research and factory farming. Others take a more pragmatic approach, insisting that the ever-increasing demand for better medicines and more food should take priority over the rights of animals.

However, few in Britain today would argue against the need to protect animals from suffering and there are many organisations which continue to campaign vigorously for animal rights.

Background

Britain could claim to be something of a world leader in animal welfare, having been responsible for the first ever animal welfare legislation and the first animal welfare charity.

In 1822 the 'Act to Prevent the Cruel and Improper Treatment of Cattle' was steered through the House of Commons by Irish MP Richard Martin – known as 'Humanity Dick' because of his campaigning for both animal and human rights.

The act stated that if any person or persons 'shall wantonly and cruelly beat, abuse, or ill-treat any horse, mare, gelding, mule, ass, ox, cow, heifer, steer, sheep, or other cattle' they would be fined a sum 'not exceeding five pounds, not less than ten shillings'; failure to pay the fine would result in a prison sentence of up to three months.

Not everyone appeared to take the new law seriously, however, and there were concerns that the legislation was not being properly implemented. Consequently, in order to provide greater protection for animals, Richard Martin, together with the Reverend Arthur Broome and fellow MP and slave trade abolitionist William Wilberforce, founded the world's first animal welfare charity, the Society for the Prevention of Cruelty to Animals (SPCA), in a London coffee shop in 1824.

The charity subsequently attracted the patronage of Queen Victoria and went on to become the Royal Society for the Prevention of Cruelty to Animals (RSPCA), well-known today as one of the world's leading animal welfare organisations.

Other animal charities began to be established towards the end of the 19th century and some, like the RSPCA, are still going strong today.

The Mayhew Animal Home, for example, founded in 1886 to protect 'the lost and starving dogs and cats of London', is still rescuing and providing shelter for thousands of animals every year; and the National Canine Defence League (NCDL) set up in 1891 to protect dogs from torture and mistreatment of any kind, today operates as the Dogs Trust and has become the UK's largest dog welfare charity.

Animal experimentation also became a major issue around that time. Although live animals had been used in research for many years, it was not until the late 19th century that anti-vivisection societies began to organise concerted opposition to the practice.

Five of the societies merged in 1898 to form the British Union, which later became the British Union for the Abolition of Vivisection. Support for the movement grew rapidly and today the BUAV and many other national and international groups are continuing to campaign for an end to all animal experimentation.

The work of the various charities was supported by the introduction of further legislation which was gradually expanded to cover domestic and other animals.

The 1911 Protection of Animals Act was introduced to 'consolidate, amend, and extend certain enactments relating to Animals and to Knackers'.

The Act made it an offence of cruelty to 'cruelly beat, kick, ill-treat, over-ride, over-drive, over-load, torture, infuriate, or terrify any animal' or permit an animal to be so used; to 'convey or carry, or permit to be conveyed or carried, any animal in such manner or position as to cause that animal any unnecessary suffering'; to 'cause or assist at the fighting or baiting of any animal'; to 'administer, or cause administration of, any poisonous or injurious drug or substance to any animal; and to 'cause or permit any animal to any operation which is performed without due care and humanity'.

Any person found guilty of such an offence of cruelty would be liable to a fine 'not exceeding twenty-five pounds'; and/or be imprisoned, 'with or without hard labour', for a term 'not exceeding six months'.

Further Acts were passed throughout the 20th century. These included the Performing Animals (Regulation) Act 1925; the Pet Animals Act 1951 (amended 1983); the Animal Boarding Establishments Act 1963; the Riding Establishments Act 1964 and 1970; and the Breeding and Sale of Dogs (Welfare) Act 1999, which amended and extended the provisions of the Breeding of Dogs Act 1973 and the Breeding of Dogs Act 1991.

In 2006 the most significant piece of animal welfare legislation was passed. The Animal Welfare Act (in force April 2007) largely repealed and replaced the 1911 Protection of Animals Act, strengthened and updated the provisions of that Act, and consolidated and updated several other pieces of animal welfare legislation.

'Animal welfare seems to attract more controversy than almost any other issue'

In addition, the Act introduced a new offence of failing to ensure the welfare of an animal. Any person responsible for an animal must ensure that five specific needs of the animal are met:

⇨ its need for a suitable environment,

⇨ its need for a suitable diet,

⇨ its need to be able to exhibit normal behaviour patterns,

⇨ any need it has to be housed with, or apart from, other animals, and

⇨ its need to be protected from pain, suffering, injury and disease.

The Act also made it an offence to dock the whole or any part of a dog's tail, unless that dog is a certified working dog of not more than five days old.

Anyone found guilty of offences under the Act could be banned from owning animals, fined up to £20,000 and/or given a prison sentence.

The Animal Welfare Act also provides for secondary legislation and codes of practice to be introduced to further promote the welfare of animals. The Government has already introduced codes of practice for the welfare of dogs, cats, horses and primates and is continuing to review other areas where similar updates could be made.

European animal welfare legislation is based on the recognition that all animals, from pets to farm animals, are sentient beings – i.e. they have powers of perception and feeling. A legally binding protocol attached to the 1997 Treaty of Amsterdam recognised animals as 'sentient beings' and this recognition was strengthened in the Lisbon Treaty of 2009 which included animal sentience as an Article in the main body of the Treaty.

The 1998 EU Council Directive 98/58 on the protection of animals kept for farming purposes set out minimum common standards of protection for animals of all species, including fish, reptiles or amphibians, kept for the production of food, wool, skin, fur or for other farming purposes.

The Directive was transposed into UK law via the Welfare of Farmed Animals (England) Regulations 2000 (amended 2007). Although the Community legislation lays down only minimum standards, the EC has said that national governments 'may adopt more stringent rules provided they are compatible with the provisions of the Treaty'. Specific rules continue to apply to laying hens, calves, pigs and broilers.

In 2006 the European Commission presented its first Action Plan on the Protection and Welfare of Animals which mapped out the Commission's planned animal welfare initiatives for 2006–2010. The Commission is currently preparing its second EU strategy for the Protection and Welfare of Animals 2011–2015 which is scheduled to be adopted in December 2011.

However, several animal welfare organisations and individuals remain concerned that animals

in other parts of the world do not have the same kind of legislative protection and are supporting a campaign, organised by the World Society for the Protection of Animals (WSPA), to secure a commitment at the United Nations for a Universal Declaration on Animal Welfare (UDAW).

'Anyone found guilty of offences under the Act could be banned from owning animals'

The UDAW would be an international agreement that animals are sentient beings, that animal welfare needs must be respected and that animal cruelty must end. The campaign is reported to have over two million supporters worldwide and the WSPA believes that securing such a commitment at the UN would create the required pressure for governments to put in place firm laws and enforcement for animal welfare.

Controversies

Animal welfare and animal rights seem to attract more controversy than almost any other issues, one of the most obvious examples being the antithetical views of vegans and livestock farmers.

Vegans believe that animals are intelligent creatures capable of feeling pain and are 'not ours to eat'. They oppose the use of all animal products and claim that vegan or vegetarian diets are more healthy and nutritious. They also believe that rearing animals for food is bad for the environment and inefficient and suggest that world food shortages could be solved by farming crops rather than animals.

However, vegans and vegetarians are still in a minority in the UK and the demand for meat and dairy products shows little sign of diminishing. Nevertheless there is a growing interest in the way food is produced and the treatment of animals in that process.

This has been largely a response to disturbing reports about the cruel treatment of animals in 'factory farming' – one of the most controversial and emotive issues – where the maximum number of animals are crammed into the minimum amount of space, unable to move freely, denied any kind of normal life and reduced to nothing more than products on a factory production line.

Horrific reports of hens trapped in tiny wire cages piled one on top of another forced unnaturally to lay the maximum amount of eggs; thousands of chickens crammed into one small shed, fattened up quickly to obtain the maximum amount of chicken meat; breeding pigs kept in small metal crates, etc., have all resulted in more consumers calling for ethically-sourced products, a cause taken up by celebrity chefs such as Hugh Fearnley-Whittingstall and Jamie Oliver.

Relentless campaigning by animal welfare organisations has had some success. The entire European Union is phasing out battery cages by 2012 and several Directives have been issued for adoption by member states in relation to improving the welfare of calves, chickens and pigs, with provision for further measures to be introduced in the future.

Proposals for large-scale dairy farms are also opposed. Following a year of intense campaigning by groups and individuals, a plan for a 3,770 cow 'mega dairy' in Nocton, Lincolnshire was finally withdrawn in February 2011 after objections were raised by the Environment Agency.

Farmers, however, are adamant that animal welfare is a priority for them. The National Farmers Union has said that factory farming 'is not normal' in the UK and suggests that the Red Tractor assurance scheme, launched in 2000 to raise standards right across the food chain, is 'a proven indicator of good animal welfare compliance'.

The Red Tractor kitemark now appears on billions of packs of meat, poultry and dairy products and is intended to reassure consumers that these products have been produced to the highest

standards of animal welfare and environmental protection.

Another highly emotive and controversial issue is animal experimentation, whether that involves testing cosmetics and household products on animals, or using animals in medical research. Opponents believe that it is ethically unacceptable for animals to suffer physical or psychological pain during these tests.

They also argue that because of the differences between humans and other animal species, test results can be misleading. The Dr Hadwen Trust for Humane Research claims that 'in some instances, reliance on inaccurate animal "models" of human disease have undoubtedly delayed medical progress'.

Proponents, however, insist that animal research has played, and is continuing to play, a vital role in treating and preventing many illnesses and diseases once thought incurable. Nevertheless, research is continuing into finding new ways to further promote the 3Rs scheme – to 'reduce, refine and replace' the use of animals in research.

The fur trade is another cause of concern for animal welfare

supporters. Although fur farming is banned in the UK, fur products can still be sold here. However, fur coats are no longer the must-have fashion item they once were following an intensive anti-fur campaign by animal welfare groups. Many high-profile celebrities and fashion designers have rejected fur and several stores now refuse to stock fur products.

'Horrific reports of hens trapped in tiny wire cages piled one on top of another'

Nevertheless the fur trade appears to be thriving, with several international designers still featuring fur in their collections. The British Fur Trade Association (BFTA) believes that 'wild or farmed, fur is a natural, renewable and sustainable resource that is kind to the environment and respectful of animals' welfare'. The BFTA is a member of the International Fur Trade Federation (IFTF), which claims to 'promote strict codes of practice that meet or exceed established and accepted animal welfare standards for wild and farmed fur'. Both the BFTA and

IFTF 'strongly condemn cruelty to animals and do not trade in endangered species'.

But Animal Defenders International claims that animals raised on fur farms or trapped in the wild are subject to 'very cruel methods'. According to ADI, 'what is of paramount concern to the fur farmers is not the welfare of the animals, but the preservation of their fur and through these methods, although incredibly painful for the animals, the fur is kept intact'.

And despite the BFTA and IFTF insisting that they 'strongly condemn trade in endangered species', the ADI remains concerned that threatened species are being illegally poached and traded for their skins, contributing to the extinction of species such as tigers, leopards and ocelots.

These concerns are shared by the International Fund for Animal Welfare and the charity believes that the Internet has created new challenges in the fight against trade in endangered species. The IFWA is calling for 'robust domestic legislation' and an international action plan to tackle illegal wildlife trade on the Internet.

' "status dogs" often suffer violence at the hands of their owners and are forced to take part in fights'

Several organisations are also campaigning for a complete ban on the use of wild animals in circuses, arguing that the conditions in which the animals are kept, the training techniques to which they are subjected, and the tricks they are forced to perform, are demeaning, cruel and inappropriate for animals of this kind.

Following a public consultation exercise in 2010 with animal welfare organisations and the circus industry, the Government decided against a ban, and instead published a 'tough new licensing scheme' in May 2011, which Defra said would ensure that any circuses in England wishing to show wild animals 'will need to demonstrate that they meet high animal welfare standards' before they are granted a licence to keep those animals.

However, this failed to satisfy campaigners and in June 2011 a backbench business debate tabled by a Conservative MP, which had cross-party support, resulted in a unanimous vote in favour of a ban. Consequently, MPs and campaigners are now pressing the Government to reconsider its decision in light of the vote and introduce a ban some time next year.

Animal welfare organisations are equally concerned about domestic wild animals which are often regarded as pests or predators by farmers and land owners. Badger culling to control the spread of bovine tuberculosis is one of the main controversies. Bovine TB is a major problem for farmers, but a recent long-term review has concluded that culling is ineffective and suggests vaccination is a better long-term solution. This view is supported by the Badger Trust which believes that the way forward is an injectable and/or an oral vaccine for badgers and also ideally a vaccine for cattle.

Deer stalking, fox snaring and the trapping of wild birds and mammals are all equally controversial and fiercely opposed by animal welfare organisations. But the British Association for Shooting and Conservation argues that pest and predator control is a necessary and integral part of conservation and wildlife management. However, the BASC also stresses that 'it is the responsibility of all those involved in pest and predator control to ensure their methods are legal, humane and carried out with sensitivity and respect for other countryside users'.

Domestic pets, in particular dogs, are often the subject of controversy, the most recent being 'handbag dogs' and 'status dogs'.

The current fashion started by 'celebrities' for carrying bichon frise, chihuahuas, shih tzus and other tiny dogs in handbags has been strongly criticised by animal charities who warn that the dogs' ability to behave normally is being restricted, which can in turn lead to behavioural problems. According to The Blue Cross, the number of miniature dogs given up or abandoned has more than tripled in the past five years.

So-called 'status dogs' such as Rottweillers and Staffordshire Bull Terriers are bought to give their owners a tougher image; they are also used for dog fighting and to intimidate other people. In addition to concerns about human safety, the RSPCA reports that these 'status dogs' often suffer violence at the hands of their owners and are forced to take part in fights which result in the dogs sustaining serious injuries.

The Dangerous Dogs Act Study Group (DDASG) and Lord Redesdale, who are supporting the Dog Control Bill currently going

'Creating a picture to the general public that certain breeds of dog are dangerous and others not is hugely irresponsible'

through Parliament, have criticised the Government for what they see as its part in the ongoing problem of 'status dogs' by making them appeal to those wishing to intimidate others and rebel against the existing law.

Lord Redesdale said: 'Banning the Pit Bull Terrier in 1991 was a huge mistake. Creating a picture to the general public that certain breeds of dog are dangerous and others not is hugely irresponsible.' The Dog Control Bill intends to repeal previous dangerous dogs acts and move the emphasis away from problem breeds to focus on owner responsibility.

⇨ Information from politics.co.uk. Please visit www.politics.co.uk for further information.

The Animal Welfare Act 2006

Information from the RSPCA.

The Animal Welfare Act 2006 only applies to vertebrate, non-human animals (e.g. mammals, birds, reptiles, amphibians and fish).

The categories of animals protected by the Act depend on the offence in question.

Protected animals are those that are:

⇨ commonly domesticated in the British Islands (e.g. dogs and cats, including feral cats and stray dogs), or

⇨ under the control of man, whether on a permanent basis (e.g. circuses and zoos) or a temporary basis (e.g. animals caught in traps), or

⇨ not living in a wild state (e.g. animals that escape from captivity but cannot be described as living in a wild state because they are non-native to the British Islands).

The Act does not apply to invertebrates (e.g. insects, shellfish, octopuses and snails), foetal or embryonic animals, wild animals (that do not fall within the definition of protected animal) and research animals that are regulated by the Animals (Scientific Procedures) Act 1986.

The Act does not apply to the sea, only to inland waters (rivers, streams, lakes) and estuaries. The Act will not affect hunting, shooting and sea fishing, and does not apply to angling.

The offences in the Act are divided into two broad categories – the promotion of animal welfare and the prevention of harm to animals.

The promotion of animal welfare

The welfare offence/'duty of care'

The owner of an animal is always considered to be legally 'responsible' for the animal's welfare. But legal responsibility (the duty of care) may also include the person who is in charge of an animal, even temporarily. If an animal is looked after by a child under 16, the person who has the care and control of the child (e.g. parent/guardian) is treated as responsible for the animal.

A person commits the welfare offence if he/she does not take reasonable steps to ensure that the needs of an animal for which he/she is responsible are met.

The Act defines an animal's needs as including:

⇨ its need for a suitable environment

⇨ its need for a suitable diet

⇨ its need to be able to exhibit normal behaviour patterns

⇨ any need it has to be housed with, or apart from, other animals

⇨ its need to be protected from pain, suffering, injury and disease.

Selling animals to persons under 16

It is illegal to sell an animal to any person whom you have reasonable cause to believe to be under 16. This includes transferring or agreeing to transfer ownership of an animal (e.g. giving an unwanted pet to someone under 16).

Offering a person under 16 the chance to win an animal as a prize

Generally, it is an offence to offer a person under 16, who is not accompanied by an adult, an animal as a prize.

The prevention of harm to animals

Unnecessary suffering

There are two separate offences:

1. to cause unnecessary suffering to a protected animal by an act (e.g. kicking a dog) or failure to act (e.g. to provide veterinary treatment)

2. to permit unnecessary suffering to an animal for which that person is responsible, which has been caused by another person (e.g. allowing someone to neglect a pet by not feeding it).

Mutilation

Mutilation, i.e. interference with the sensitive tissues or bone structure of protected animals, is banned unless:

⇨ it is necessary for the animal's medical treatment, or

⇨ it is a procedure specifically allowed by regulations because it is performed in the animal's long-term welfare interest or it is an accepted method of animal management, e.g. on a farm.

Docking of dogs' tails

It is illegal to dock a dog's tail unless this is required for the purpose of its medical treatment or the dog is a certified working dog of a certain breed or breed type (as specified by secondary legislation) and is not more than five days old.

The showing of dogs with docked tails is also restricted. It is an offence to show a dog whose tail has been wholly or partially removed on or after 28 March 2007 (Wales) or 6 April 2007 (England) at an event that people pay money to watch. However, it is not illegal if the dog is a certified working dog and is shown only for the purposes of demonstrating its working ability.

Administration of poisons, etc.

There are three separate offences relating to the administration of poisonous or injurious substances or drugs. An example of what is covered includes leaving rat poison out, which may be eaten by another animal.

Fighting, etc.

An animal fight is defined as an occasion on which a protected animal is placed with an animal or a human for the purpose of fighting, wrestling or baiting.

There are a number of offences relating to animal fights. The main offences include causing an animal to fight, or

attempting to do so, receiving money for admission to a fight, publicising a fight, training an animal to fight, betting on a fight and being present at an animal fight without lawful authority.

Animals commonly used for fighting include dogs, cockerels and badgers.

Sanctions

The magistrates have a range of sanctions available to them in the event of finding someone guilty of offences under the Act. Depending on the offence, these may include:

⇨ custodial sentences of up to six months

⇨ deprivation orders (taking the animal away)

⇨ disqualification orders (banning a person from owning, keeping, controlling, influencing, dealing or transporting animals)

⇨ fines of up to £20,000

⇨ destruction of the animal.

Associated secondary legislation and codes of practice

The Animal Welfare Act has been designed to evolve over time and have a positive impact on attitudes to animals. Secondary legislation and codes of practice on issues such as racing greyhounds, wild animals in circuses, performing animals, commercial pet vending, keeping primates as pets, keeping cats and dogs and rearing of game birds are expected in the next couple of years.

Until these are in place, any animal may be used for any purpose or activity, provided it is lawful (section 9.3). At times, this may appear to be in opposition to the welfare offence; for example, the suffering of battery hens. However, the standard to which the 'duty of care' applies is the extent required by 'good practice'.

Only the courts are entitled to define what good practice means in relation to looking after different animals, but because the Act is so new they haven't had much opportunity to do this yet.

The concept of good practice is not static – it may evolve with time. For example, it is currently common practice to keep rabbits in hutches on their own. The Act does not make this practice illegal. However, an increasing number of experts believe that rabbits are social animals that, in a natural state, live in groups, and that living alone does not fulfil their need to have the company of other animals. Therefore, the courts may, in the future, decide on the basis of such advice that keeping a rabbit on its own is not good practice and is therefore a breach of the welfare offence.

⇨ The above information is reprinted with kind permission from the RSPCA. Please visit www.rspca.co.uk for further information on this and other subjects.

Questions and answers about factory farming

Phillip Lymbery, Chief Executive of Compassion in World Farming, answers your questions about factory farming.

What is factory farming?

I take factory farming to mean the close confinement of farmed animals in cages, crates or overcrowded sheds or barren outdoor feedlots. This includes, for example, chickens kept in battery cages to produce eggs, chickens confined in broiler sheds for their meat, and pigs kept in barren pens for their meat. Animals in factory farms are treated more like production machines than individual sentient beings with welfare needs. These animals are specially bred for purpose. They are fast growing or high producing breeds. They are vulnerable to painful production-related health problems. Factory farms are energy-intensive and use concentrated feed (such as soya and cereals), high mechanisation and minimal labour.

Which countries use factory farming?

Various kinds of factory farming are banned in a few countries (e.g. Norway and Switzerland) and some kinds, e.g. barren battery cages, in Germany and Austria. There are measures being taken to phase out some factory farming systems, e.g. battery cages throughout Europe in 2012. However, as a general rule, factory farming is practised throughout the world.

Why is factory farming so bad?

I believe factory farming is bad for animal welfare, for the health of consumers who eat intensively-farmed meat and dairy products and for the environment because of the pollution it causes. It's bad for animal welfare because the animals are caged or confined. Factory farms are unnatural environments to keep animals. Consequently, they cause what I call self-induced problems. For example, chickens are debeaked to stop them from pecking each other; but beak trimming is unnecessary in well managed free range systems. Factory farming is bad for consumers because we eat too much meat and dairy products, which are a major source of saturated fat in the diet. Experts recommend reducing consumption of animal products to lower the risk of heart disease, obesity, type 2 diabetes and certain cancers. Our research shows we can feed the world without factory farming and address global warming!

Is antibiotic use in farming really such a problem?

I'm very concerned about this. Keeping very large numbers of chickens and pigs, for example, in close confinement creates the ideal conditions for the rapid spread of disease. Overcrowding can also lead to stress, which can weaken the animals' ability to fight infections. This is why antibiotics are used and misused by farmers and agribusiness throughout the world. The Soil Association and Compassion co-signed a letter to then Prime Minister Gordon Brown calling on the Government to act in response to a report produced by the Chief Medical Officer which detailed the problem of antimicrobial resistance being transferred from farm animals to humans.

Do all factory farmed chickens really have such a bad life?

Yes, they do. Chickens kept for meat production have been bred to grow so quickly that many of them suffer from painful lameness or die of heart failure. Their short lives are spent in overcrowded sheds where they have no option but to sit or stand in their own waste. Hens kept for laying are imprisoned in cages with less space than the area of one sheet of writing paper each. Nothing about their life is natural. They cannot fulfil their behavioural and psychological needs to, for example, forage for food, dust bathe and stretch their wings. Life in a factory farm is not anything I would wish on anyone.

Is it true that many animals reared in factory farms die as a result of their conditions? How many of them actually make it to become 'meat'?

The financial economies of scale in factory farming are such that it is cost effective for agribusiness to write off as an affordable expense the loss of life of a significant number of animals or birds which occurs in the time they are raised before slaughter. Mortality rates vary from one farm to another, but it is typical for around 5% of factory-farmed chickens to die before reaching slaughter weight. In a shed of 10,000 birds that means around 500 of them die or need to be culled before they even make it to six weeks of age. Chickens would naturally live for up to seven years or more.

How would you explain to a starving family in Africa that animal welfare is of any importance?

With a billion people hungry in the world, the priority is to see that they are fed. However, factory farming is not the solution for feeding the hungry.

'factory farming is not the solution for feeding the hungry'

Many developing world farmers depend on their animals for their living and the production of cheap meat often undermines their livelihood. Meanwhile, the feeding of grain to factory farmed animals is hugely wasteful of food that could be put to much better use feeding people directly. Factory farming also fuels demand for grain and soya, thereby pushing up global prices for basic foodstuffs. There is a real danger from this that the poorest people will be less able to afford basic food items like bread.

The bottom line is that treating animals badly through factory farming has impacts detrimentally on our environment, public health and our ability to feed people. Therefore, animal welfare and human well-being are very much interlinked.

We need humane and sustainable solutions to solve problems of food security globally. Josphat Ngonyo, Head of the African Network for Farm Animals, puts it like this: 'We must acknowledge that as human beings we share the planet together with fellow non-human beings, the animals. Like us, they suffer hunger, thirst, pain and injury. They can become fearful, suffer from diseases, be uncomfortable and feel distressed. Thus, we need to appreciate them as fellow beings that we co-exist with on earth.'

How can I make sure that I only buy animal produce that has come from compassionately reared animals?

I look for free range and organic products, particularly the Soil Association's Organic Certification as this scheme has high welfare standards. For those on a budget, the RSCPA's Freedom Foods scheme offers higher indoor and outdoor standards than the industry norm. I'm wary of the Red Tractor as food produced on factory farms can be certified by this. I don't automatically trust products which use words such as 'farm assured', 'farm fresh', 'locally sourced' and 'produced to high animal welfare standards'.

⇨ The above information is reprinted with kind permission from Compassion in World Farming. Please visit www.acompassionateworld.org for further information on this and other subjects.

© Compassion in World Farming

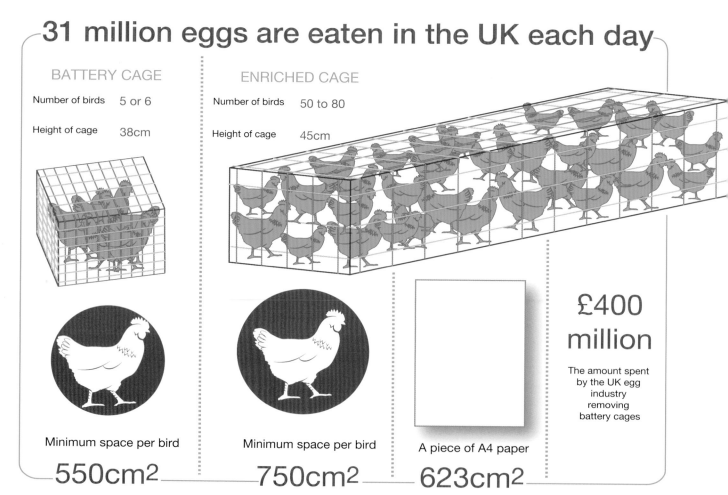

31 million eggs are eaten in the UK each day

BATTERY CAGE

Number of birds   5 or 6

Height of cage   38cm

ENRICHED CAGE

Number of birds   50 to 80

Height of cage   45cm

£400 million

The amount spent by the UK egg industry removing battery cages

Minimum space per bird

550cm2

Minimum space per bird

750cm2

A piece of A4 paper

623cm2

Source: The above diagram is reproduced with permission from The Independent. © The Independent

We don't need mega-dairies

A new report on UK dairy farming has concluded that it is possible to produce milk at a profit on all sizes of farm. What's more, it found the amount of milk each cow produces isn't the key factor in making a profit.

These findings mean huge zero-graze dairies, where cows are pushed to their limit to produce ever higher amounts of milk, aren't necessary for dairy farmers to make money. That damages the credibility of the 'bigger is better' argument for zero-graze mega-dairies with high yielding cows.

Profiting from efficient milk production

The report, *Profiting from efficient milk production*, was produced by Dairy Co. It outlines the key findings of its milkbench and programme, which allows farmers to benchmark their dairy's performance against others.

It concludes: 'Milk can be produced efficiently from any of the major systems that are currently practised in Britain. Moreover, efficient milk production is possible at almost any scale of production.'

Cows belong in fields

This makes encouraging reading for everyone who believes, like Compassion in World Farming, that cows belong in fields, as it confirms industrial dairying is not the only viable model for dairy farming in the UK. Traditional dairy farming, where cows are allowed outside to graze on pasture, is just as economically feasible.

Compassion's CEO Philip Lymbery explains: 'There is ample evidence that a cow's welfare is better served by being pasture fed in the field, that's where they belong, after all. With this new report saying it's just as viable, there's really no need to consider keeping cows indoors all year round.

'We can have a humane and sustainable dairy industry that is profitable.'

> **'Cows belong in fields, there is no economic reason why they shouldn't stay there'**

The report says that 'Average yield per cow is not the main driver of profit', which is particularly encouraging, as pushing cows to produce ever-higher quantities of milk is damaging to their welfare.

As a scientific opinion from the European Food Safety Authority (EFSA) says: 'Long term genetic selection for high milk yield is the major factor causing poor welfare, in particular health problems, in dairy cows.'

And the extensive data collected by Dairy Co prove that cows do not need to be pushed to their physical limit in order for a dairy farmer to run a profitable farm.

'If dairy cows are not kept on pasture for parts of the year ... there is an increased risk of lameness, hoof problems, teat tramp and some bacterial infections'

Perhaps one of the most heartening conclusions of the market assessment is that the cost of production is key to profit.

A report by the Beyond Calf Exports Stakeholders Forum, of which Compassion is a member, shows feed costs (one of the major costs of dairy farming) are lower in robust, lower yielding dairy cows, which can be fed on pasture.

The Forum report also showed the culling rate was lower in herds of lower yielding cows allowed to graze in fields and replacement costs are another major factor in the cost of production.

Compassion's campaign against the Nocton Dairies proposal last year, which won us an Observer Ethical Campaigner of the Year award, was firmly based on the conviction that access to well managed pasture wherever possible is essential to dairy cow welfare.

Put in other words, EFSA say: 'If dairy cows are not kept on pasture for parts of the year, i.e. they are permanently on a zero-grazing system, there is an increased risk of lameness, hoof problems, teat tramp, mastitis, metritis, dystocia, ketosis, retained placenta and some bacterial infections.'

Compassion welcomes the *Profiting from efficient milk production* report as a valuable contribution to the essential debate on dairy farming in this country and further proof that industrial dairying is not inevitable.

Cows belong in fields, there is no economic reason why they shouldn't stay there.

⇨ The above information is reprinted with kind permission from Compassion in World Farming. Please visit www.ciwf.org.uk for further information on this and other subjects.

© Compassion in World Farming

Super farms are needed in UK, says leader of National Farmers Union

Britain urged to ape countries such as the US and Saudi Arabia and build farms housing tens of thousands of cows or pigs.

By Juliette Jowit, political correspondent

The president of the National Farmers Union believes the UK needs more and bigger 'super farms' to keep food prices from rising too high and to maintain high animal welfare standards. Peter Kendall gave his views as figures reportedly showed that the lack of farmland in Britain was now as acute as the shortfall in China.

Proposals for the first livestock farms that would breed thousands of animals have been dubbed mega farms by critics who claim they will create mass herds in sterile conditions where injuries will go unnoticed, disease will spread quickly and the environment will struggle to cope with the slurry and pollution.

But, as planning experts continue to consider at least two planning applications for large-scale pig and dairy farms, Kendall said that more super farms would be created and the Government should make adjustments to allow some farms to keep several thousand animals and be part of a trial aimed at helping Britain feed its population as food demand rises around the world.

The problem thought to be facing Britain is highlighted by figures from the Agriculture and Horticulture Development Board showing that, though Britain has about 5% of China's 1.3 billion population, it has less than 3% of its land area.

An independent report by the Parliamentary Office of Science and Technology (POST) found that much larger farms than those in Britain could be 'both good and bad' for animal welfare and the environment, arguing that they could 'potentially' improve conditions for animals and the protection of the environment.

'The challenge of feeding everybody with the constraints of climate change and weather shocks is so great we'll need a complete rethink,' said Kendall.

Although livestock farms in the UK have been consolidating for many years, POST's report, entitled *Livestock Super Farms,* found that typically the units held 100 to 150 head of cattle or pigs.

Even the biggest UK farms are dwarfed by the mega farms of other countries. In the US, farms with 10,000 pigs are not uncommon and Saudi Arabia has a super dairy with a herd of 37,000.

In Britain last year, there was a move to house 8,000 dairy cows at Nocton, Lincolnshire. This application from Nocton Dairies was withdrawn because of official concerns about water pollution and the animal welfare protest that took place at Westminster in 2010.

Two more scaled-up proposals are being considered. These are a farm for 2,500 sows and their piglets at Foston, Derbyshire, and another for 1,000 cows in Powys, Wales.

Last year, too, a government report on the future of food and farming stated that 'the global food supply must be increased through sustainable intensification' to cope with population increase, climate change and other factors. Ministers are now waiting to hear from a working group on the subject.

POST records large farms in the UK, but perhaps because they have grown piecemeal, or been split between various land holdings, they have not attracted any high-profile attention from animal rights and environment campaigners.

Concerns about large-scale animal farming fall into four categories: of animal welfare; of super units destroying small farms and rural communities; of farms straining soil and water resources and requiring mass transport of chemicals, generating more greenhouse gas pollution; and of such units being unsightly and emitting foul smells.

Kendall said the UK was about 62% self-sufficient in the food it could produce overall and 40% self-sufficient with regard to pork – so there was 'plenty of scope' for big producers while still leaving room for smaller ones.

At the heart of Kendall's defence of super farms is his belief that bigger farms are more profitable (or less loss-making) so can afford better equipment, more space and experts able 'to protect the environment and animals'.

He highlighted the Foston application, from Midland Pig Producers, which proposed building an abattoir near the farm so the pigs would not have to travel far to slaughter.

The plan was also to fit equipment to trap ammonia and other gasses to protect local residents and to generate 'renewable' electricity and heat. The applicants had promised to achieve the RSPCA's Freedom Food accreditation for animal welfare.

Kendall argued that farmers running large units would generally be able to afford to employ veterinarians and other experts such as nutritionists, and to attract other operations to local areas, such as ethanol plants generating high-quality protein waste that could be used as feed.

'I want to make sure we're not importing food that's produced to lower welfare standards and therefore driving our farmers out.'

He envisaged more farms on the scale of Foston or the Powys proposal. Much bigger operations, similar to the withdrawn Nocton scheme, could be tried out, he said, though he did not think that would become the norm, principally because it was hard to find locations far enough away from population centres.

'This is about a few experimental versions, so we can see whether it lowers greenhouse gas emissions, see whether it's welfare friendly, see what the impacts are on the environment.'

Compassion in World Farming (CWF) said it was deeply uncomfortable about mega farms, particularly since they usually relied on animals being kept indoors.

Joyce D'Silva, CWF's director of public affairs, said there was 'good scientific evidence' showing it was better for farm animals to go outside, and that it was harder for workers to pick out lame or ill animals kept in the thousands.

'We see each animal as an individual sentient being,' D'Silva said. 'The market would put animals in thousands: it's hard to treat them as individuals.'

5 June 2012

⇨ The above article originally appeared in the *Guardian* and is reprinted with permission. Please visit www.guardian.co.uk for further information.

Farming in numbers

- 110 = average dairy herd in the UK
- 8,000 = cows in original application for Nocton super dairy
- 37,000 = size of herd at a mega dairy farm in Saudi Arabia
- 148 = average number of sows on a UK pig farm
- 2,500 = pigs that would be housed in new farm at Foston
- 10,000 = pigs at a US mega farm

An outrage in Belfast: the sad case of Lennox, the dog

Article by Joan K. Smith for The Huffington Post.

Those of us living in what we consider free societies often feel secure that if we comply by laws, pay our taxes, and maintain other civic duties we should not live in fear of government officials entering our homes and disrupting our families.

Not so in Belfast, Northern Ireland, where a tragic situation that is nothing short of Orwellian has played out for over two years. Lennox, a Labrador/American Bulldog mix, was seized from the Barnes family under the UK's Dangerous Dogs Act (DDA) and sentenced to death due simply to his physical measurements. Under the DDA, if a dog's measurements are in line with their standard for 'pit bull types', the dog can be seized without warrant and sentenced to death (a recent amendment stipulates the that the dog must also be proven dangerous). The DDA assumption that physical traits dictate a dog's behavioural tendencies is contradicted by well known dog experts and virtually every major veterinary, animal control, and emergency medical associations worldwide – all of whom have spoken out against these laws.

It's hard to imagine a more unlikely target for the law than the Barnes family. Lennox is an American Bulldog/Labrador mix who had never been reported for any act of aggression, and in fact had never exhibited a single sign of misbehaviour. He is not only a family pet, but has served as a therapy dog and soulmate for a disabled girl, Brook Barnes, who is now 13. Lennox's family had provided a stable, loving home environment. He had been microchipped, neutered, DNA registered, insured, and even had a valid city-issued dog licence.

By all accounts, Caroline Barnes, a former veterinary nurse, is a model pet owner.

Yet on 19 May 2010, the City of Belfast saw fit to turn their world upside down, in the most baffling way imaginable: Two dog wardens (who operate under the auspices of Belfast City Council) came knocking at the Barnes door bearing a warrant with an entirely different address; it's still unclear whether the visit was a simple mistake or prompted by Ms Barnes recently renewing the city dog licence. The Barnes related that after smoking cigarettes and pleasantly chatting over tea, they produced a tape with which they measured Lennox; they then announced they were seizing him because, by their assessment of his measurements, he was 'of type'.

That was nearly two years ago. Since then, in spite of massive worldwide outcry, including pleas from noted dog behavioural experts and celebrities, a petition that now bears over 127,000 signatures, and a growing 'Boycott Belfast' movement, Lennox has been held in a secret location while the family pitches a desperate legal battle for his life.

It's no exaggeration to say that the prosecution case against Lennox has been rife with inconsistencies, errors, and even accusations of perjury. The absurd twists and cast of characters could make this case darkly comic – Samuel Butler or Dickens would have had a romp with it – if it didn't ultimately hinge on one innocent life, and the suffering of a heartbroken girl.

One would think the case would have been put to bed in September 2011, after two expert animal behaviourists, Sarah Fisher and David Ryan, presented the results of their separate, extensive evaluations of Lennox. Both came to the conclusion that Lennox is friendly and of no danger, and presented these reports to the court.

Inexplicably, the judge dismissed those evaluations, and instead relied on the opinion of one Peter Tallack, a police dog handler and noted supporter of the DDA, whose official role in the case was simply 'breed identifier'. In a quirky bit of testimony, a flustered Tallack offered the opinion that Lennox was 'waiting to go off'.

Apparently using this as the basis, Judge Rodgers called Lennox 'a disaster waiting to happen' in a ruling that upheld Lennox's death sentence not on the basis of any past or current behaviour, but on a projection that he might be aggressive at some point in the future. (Imagine if a human defendant were convicted on these grounds!)

When the defence appealed again in late January of this year, the case was reviewed by the very same

Judge Rodgers, who – surprise – chose not to overturn his own ruling.

Outrage sums up the reaction of Victoria Stilwell, celebrity dog trainer and host of the programme *It's Me or the Dog,* with whom I spoke earlier this year. Stilwell has been outspoken in her support for Lennox, devoting a number of articles and a podcast to it, and against breed-specific legislation in general (which she sums up as 'addressing the wrong end of the leash'). Stilwell has studied the video assessments of Lennox and reviewed Sarah Fisher's report, and simply can't believe the judge would have taken the word of Tallack – who is, by his own admission, not a behaviourist – over the opinions of two highly regarded professionals.

Concurring with Stilwell is Jim Crosby, a dog trainer and expert in canine aggression. By his account, he has personally assessed more dogs involved in fatal attacks than anyone else on the planet. He stresses that breed is most certainly not a factor in determining whether a dog is dangerous or not; it is the individual characteristics of a dog. This is a man who knows aggressive animals, and he cries foul in the Lennox case. 'This poor dog didn't do anything, he was minding his own business, happily at home,' he said in a January conversation. 'That's the baffling thing.'

Also like Stilwell, Crosby questions why the testimony of Tallack, a police dog handler, was given credence by the judge. He says to have someone with Tallack's highly focused skill set evaluate a family dog like Lennox for aggressive tendencies is 'like asking a guy who works on Piper plane to repair the space shuttle'. It's a very different type of dog in a completely different situation.

Both Stilwell and Crosby continue to speak out passionately about the Lennox case, and Stilwell has especially expressed alarm over evidence that Lennox's health is deteriorating further, based on photo evidence showing massive hair loss and sores.

A final appeal to high court is set for 24 May. If it is ruled that Lennox cannot be returned to his family, the defence is asking at least to allow a friendly party in the Republic of Ireland (where there is no breed-specific legislation) to adopt him. Meanwhile, somewhere in Belfast, a family's beloved pet – a dog who has never spent so much as a day in a boarding kennel – remains locked in a small dank cell surrounded by sawdust and faeces, a victim of misused policy and a few humans who would rather see him put to death than admit a mistake. Now, that's a crime.

9 May 2012

⇨ Information from *The Huffington Post*. Please visit www.huffingtonpost.com for further information.

Olympic opening plans branded 'wholly irresponsible'

Information from Captive Animals' Protection Society

Leading animal protection charity, the Captive Animals' Protection Society (CAPS), has today spoken out against plans to recreate a rural landscape including live animals within the Olympic Stadium at the opening event of this summer's games. The charity labelled the event, designed by acclaimed director, Danny Boyle, 'wholly irresponsible' and said that the plans have triggered a wave of opposition amongst its supporters and the general public.

News reports yesterday announced that 12 horses, three cows, two goats, ten chickens, ten ducks, nine geese, 70 sheep and three sheepdogs will be used as part of the event named 'Isles Of Wonder' and was immediately met with concern by organisations and individuals alike.

Said the Director of CAPS, Liz Tyson:

'With 62,000 people in attendance, the noise, the lights and the charged atmosphere, it beggars belief that the Olympic Committee is allowing this to happen. It should be obvious that this event has the potential to be terrifying for the animals involved and we are shocked to see that their welfare needs have apparently been disregarded in the name of entertainment. We have been inundated with complaints from our supporters, asking what they can do to help to stop these plans going ahead.

We are calling on the Olympic organisers to step in and ensure that the use of live animals does not happen.'

The charity has sponsored a petition to the Olympic Committee and is calling for members of the public to make their voices heard by signing up.

13 June 2012

⇨ Information from Captive Animals' Protection Society. Please visit www. captiveanimals.org.

No ban on circus animals as Cameron acts as chief whip

David Cameron was last night accused of deploying 'smoke and mirrors' to avoid imposing an immediate ban on wild animals in travelling circuses.

The Government announced plans for a licensing regime to monitor animals' well-being as a precursor to outlawing their use entirely.

But to the dismay of animal rights campaigners and MPs of all parties, it was unable to give a firm date for when a ban would be implemented.

MPs unanimously voted in favour of the move last year and surveys also suggest an overwhelming majority of the public wants the practice outlawed. More than 30,000 people signed *The Independent*'s petition last year calling for a ban.

The Department for the Environment, Food and Rural Affairs (Defra) initially supported the move, but was overruled by David Cameron.

James Paice, the Agriculture Minister, said yesterday that the Government would consult on plans for a 'tough new licensing regime which we can put in place swiftly'.

He told MPs that ministers remained 'minded' to outlaw circus animals, but would not commit himself on the timing of a ban. And the Government's impact assessment of its proposal for a licensing regime said: 'The legal issues surrounding a ban mean that pursuing a ban is not an immediate possibility.'

The Tory MP Mark Pritchard, who last year disclosed attempts by Tory whips acting on Downing Street's orders to bully him into dropping demands for a ban, dismissed the announcement as 'disingenuous'. He said: 'Without a proper commitment to legislation in this Parliament, any claim to be listening to the will of Parliament is meaningless.

'This is a classic smoke-and-mirrors tactic by Number 10. Meantime animals continue to suffer.'

2 March 2012

⇨ The article originally appeared in *The Independent*. www.independent.co.uk.

Circuses to be banned from using performing wild animals

Wild animals will no longer be made to perform in travelling circuses under proposals being developed by Defra.

The Government will seek to introduce primary legislation at the earliest opportunity to achieve its much-stated desire to ban travelling circuses from using performing wild animals.

'There is no place in today's society for wild animals being used for our entertainment in travelling circuses'

In the meantime, owners of travelling circuses will be required to meet tough new licensing standards, which will ensure high welfare conditions for wild animals, following the publication of the Government's consultation on a circus licensing scheme.

'Defra is developing proposals to realise the Government's desire to introduce a ban'

Animal Welfare Minister Lord Taylor said:

'There is no place in today's society for wild animals being used for our entertainment in travelling circuses. Wild animals deserve our respect.

'We have said many times we wanted to ban this outdated practice, but before we could do that there were serious legal issues we had to consider.

'We are developing proposals to introduce a Bill as soon as Parliamentary time allows. In the meantime we are introducing a Circus Licensing Scheme to ensure decent conditions for wild animals in travelling circuses.'

A consultation on the new welfare licences has been published today. Anyone responsible for a travelling circus that uses wild animals in a circus performance will need to hold a valid licence, meet strict welfare standards, prepare and follow plans for caring for every animal and have a retirement plan for each animal.

The proposed welfare standards will cover all aspects of life for a wild animal in a travelling circus environment, including:

⇨ Good accommodation and housing whilst being transported, at a performance, and in winter quarters;

⇨ Full veterinary care;

⇨ Controlling carefully who has access to the animals;

⇨ Diet including food storage, preparation and provision;

⇨ Environment such as noise and temperature; and

⇨ Welfare during training and performance.

The licensing scheme will be enforced through inspections by a dedicated Government-appointed inspector and paid for by the circuses. The consultation will close on 25 April 2012 and draft Regulations will be brought before Parliament by the summer.

If any circus owner decides they do not wish to keep their wild animals Defra will work with them and animal charities to help them consider the best options available, such as re-homing the animals.

A ban on ethical grounds of wild animals performing in travelling circuses requires primary legislation. Therefore Defra is developing proposals to realise the Government's desire to introduce a ban.

1 March 2012

⇨ Information from the Department for Environment Food and Rural Affairs. Please visit their website www.defra.gov.uk for further information on this and other topics.

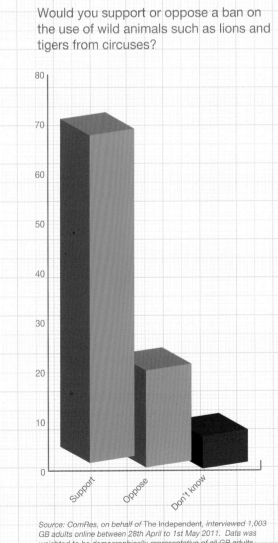

Would you support or oppose a ban on the use of wild animals such as lions and tigers from circuses?

Support — Oppose — Don't know

Source: ComRes, on behalf of The Independent, interviewed 1,003 GB adults online between 28th April to 1st May 2011. Data was weighted to be demographically representative of all GB adults. Full tables at www.comres.co.uk.

Religious slaughter

Extract from Commons Library Standard Note.

By Christopher Barclay

⇨ The Jewish method of slaughter, Shechita, requires animals not to be stunned before slaughter. Islamic food rules, for Halal meat, can be satisfied with animals stunned before slaughter if animals do not die as a result of the stun, but there is no definitive consensus and slaughter without pre-stunning does also take place.

⇨ Much of the meat on an animal killed by Shechita may not qualify as Kosher meat. There is no requirement that it should be labelled as meat from an animal killed without pre-stunning.

⇨ The Coalition Government has no intention of making Halal or Shechita slaughter illegal, but it is considering welfare labelling of meat.

⇨ Food Standards Agency figures in 2012, the first since 2003, show that more than 80% of animals are stunned before slaughter for Halal meat in the UK.

11 June 2012

⇨ The above information is reproduced with kind permission from www.parliament.co.uk.

> What is done to stop halal slaughter? It should be ILLEGAL. It used to be, but now appears to be non-pc. Why are there no TV documentaries about the living conditions of cows, horses, pigs, sheep, etc., their loading, transport and slaughter? They would wake people up and make them think.

The Muslim method of slaughtering animals for food requires that the animals are alive and healthy at the time of slaughter. Stunning has been opposed by some Muslims because of concerns that the stun may kill the animal. The purpose of stunning is to make the animal unconscious rather than to kill it but some methods of stunning may induce cardiac arrest at the same time as loss of consciousness (e.g. electrical stunning methods where the electrodes span the heart as well as the brain). However, head-only electrical stunning induces unconsciousness without stopping the heart from beating so that the animal is still alive when the throat is cut.

Following demonstrations of the reversible nature of electrical stunning applied to the head only, many Muslim authorities have accepted that this method of pre-stunning can be used in Halal slaughter. Data from the Meat Hygiene Service suggests that electrical stunning has now been routinely adopted in many Halal slaughterhouses in the UK and that the majority of animals (including poultry) slaughtered for Halal meat in the UK are now stunned. The Jewish method of slaughtering animals for food requires that the animals are healthy at the time of slaughter and that they must not have suffered any physical injury. For this reason, pre-slaughter stunning methods that are judged to cause physical injuries prior to cutting the throat have been considered unacceptable. Therefore, all poultry and the majority of mammals slaughtered for Kosher meat are not stunned and those that are only receive the stun after the throat has been cut. Slaughter without pre-stunning inflicts unnecessary pain and distress on animals and Compassion in World Farming believes that it should not be permitted. Whilst we respect the right to religious freedom, we do not believe this should extend to practices that inflict suffering on animals.

There is currently no requirement under UK or EU law for the meat from animals slaughtered without stunning to be labelled as such. Until the current exemption permitting slaughter without pre-stunning is repealed, Compassion in World Farming believes the law should require that all animals who are not pre-stunned must at least receive an immediate post-cut stun and that all meat from animals slaughtered without pre-stunning must be clearly labelled as such. The European Parliament voted in June 2010 to require compulsory labelling for all meat from animals killed without stunning. In order to become law, this would require approval by the European Commission and the Council of Ministers.

⇨ The above information is from Compassion in World Farming. Please visit www.acompassionateworld.org.

What's wrong with bullfighting?

Information from League Against Cruel Sports.

Each year tens of thousands of bulls are maimed, tortured and killed for entertainment in Spain, Portugal, France, Columbia, Mexico, Venezuela, Peru, Ecuador and the USA. Thousands of horses are also injured or killed each year in bullfights, as they are frequently used as a part of the bullfighting display.

In a typical bullfight, the animal is attacked by men on foot and on horseback with lances and harpoons. The matador forces the confused and exhausted bull to make a few charges before eventually attempting to kill it with a sword. If not killed, the animal is stabbed repeatedly until paralysed. When the bull finally collapses, its spinal cord is cut, but the animal may still be conscious as its ears and tail are cut off and kept as a trophy.

Further cruelty takes place away from the gaze of the general public. Bulls are sometimes weakened and disorientated prior to a fight, for example through drugging, or by having Vaseline smeared in their eyes to impair their vision. A bull's horns may also be shaved before a fight, making them extremely sensitive to pain.

A bullfight is never a fair fight. The animals involved suffer immensely, and all in the name of human entertainment. The League campaigns for a complete ban on this cruel and outdated 'sport'.

Bullfighting facts

The pro-bullfighting lobby would have us believe that bullfighting is an art form, and an ancient culture which must be preserved for future generations. In reality it is a cruel bloodsport which causes enormous suffering to the animals involved, and usually results in death.

⇨ An estimated 40,000 bulls are killed in Europe each year. The total number killed across the world is estimated at 250,000.

⇨ Whilst it is still legal in most parts of Spain, bullfighting is banned by law in Catalonia and in the Canary Islands.

⇨ Bullfighting is banned by law in most parts of France. However, it remains legal in parts of the south and east of the country.

⇨ Despite claims to the contrary, bullfighting is not a key economic sector. Less than 400 people are employed full-time all year round by the bullfighting industry in Spain.

⇨ Famous writers and thinkers who have opposed bullfighting include George Bernard Shaw, Franz Kafka, Mark Twain and H.G. Wells.

⇨ The European bullfighting industry receives up to 600 million Euros a year in public funding.

⇨ Recent opinion polls have shown that a significant majority of people are against bullfighting. 89% of British people would not visit a bullfight (ComRes, 2008), whilst in Spain 67% are not interested in bullfighting (Gallup, 2008). In France, 69% of people oppose public funding for bullfighting (YouGov, 2009)

⇨ Each year the European Union provides an estimated £37 million pounds in subsidies to farmers which breed bulls for bullfights.

⇨ Information from League Against Cruel Sports. Please visit www. league.uk.com for further information.

© 2011, League Against Cruel Sports

The fur trade

Information from Animal Aid.

In the UK, farming animals to kill them for their fur was banned and finally phased out in 2002. Fur farming still goes on around the world and fur garments can still legally be sold in shops in the UK. There are two simple reasons: profits and vanity. People who kill animals and make coats out of their skins make money out of it, and people who wear the coats think they look glamorous. The fur trade tries to advertise fur as 'natural' to hide the horrific and unnatural way that the animals are imprisoned on fur farms, or trapped in the wild, and then killed.

Fur farming

Worldwide, more than 40 million animals are killed for their fur – 85% are bred and killed on fur farms and the rest are trapped in the wild. This figure does not include the thousands of millions of rabbits killed for the fur trade. The most commonly bred animals on fur farms are mink and fox, but the industry also breeds and kills polecats, raccoons and chinchillas. It is estimated that two million cats and dogs are also killed for their fur. There are 6,500 fur farms in the EU. Europe is responsible for 70% of global mink fur production, and 63% of fox fur production. The countries that farm the most animals for their fur are Denmark, China and Finland.

'Why do tens of millions of fur-bearing animals die every year ... just to make fur coats?'

The conditions

On fur farms, animals are imprisoned in tiny wire-mesh cages for their entire lives until they are killed. For species such as mink and fox, these conditions are especially appalling, as they are wild animals and would naturally travel many miles each day. Being caged in huge sheds, where thousands of other animals are also imprisoned, drives them insane with anxiety and fear. Repetitive movements, such as head-bobbing and circling, are therefore common.

Methods of killing

Animals on fur farms are killed by electrocution (through the use of electrodes in the mouth and anus), gassing, lethal injection or neck breaking. These crude methods are employed to ensure that the pelts (the animals' skins and fur) are not damaged.

Fur trapping

The most commonly-used trap is the barbaric steel-jawed leghold trap. When set by the trapper, the spring-loaded jaws are opened to their fullest extent and secured with a metal clip. When an animal steps on it, the clip is released and the device snaps shut with incredible force. The intention is to catch the animal's leg, but they can also be caught across their back, neck or head. The trapped animal will be in agony, unable to escape, for hours or even days, until the trapper comes back to suffocate or beat them to death.

'Worldwide, more than 40 million animals are killed for their fur'

Leghold traps do not discriminate. They catch any animal who treads on them. Trappers call these non-target animals 'trash'. The contraptions are now banned in 88 countries, including the UK, and in several states across the USA. However, fur is still imported to the UK from animals who have been killed by leghold traps in other countries.

Fur trade arguments

Supporters of the fur industry often claim that trapping is a tool of wildlife management and conservation. This is untrue. Many species of wild cats such as ocelots, margays, lynx and Geoffrey's cat are being driven to the verge of extinction by hunting and trapping. There are only 4,000–7,000 snow leopards left in the world. Sea otters were driven to the very edge of extinction and, despite protection, their numbers remain very low. The sea mink paid the ultimate price for having a beautiful fur coat – extinction.

'Millions of wild animals are killed in traps for their fur every single year. The main countries involved are Russia, the USA and Canada'

Fur farmers try to insist that the animals are looked after very well and that they do not suffer when they are killed. Yet undercover footage shows time and again that the animals are going insane from their confinement, endlessly weaving and pacing in their desperation to be free. When they are killed, it often takes a few attempts to break the animals' necks, as they try to squirm their way out of their executioner's grip; or, if they are electrocuted, the terror as the electrodes are shoved into their mouth and anus is clear. When they cry out and their bodies convulse, there can be no doubt that these animals are dying in agony.

⇨ The above information is reprinted with kind permission from Animal Aid. Please visit www.animalaid.org.uk for further information.

Fur: the natural responsible choice

Information from British Fur Trade.

Fur is fashionable

Retail fur sales continue to rise in the UK and globally. The global fur trade is now worth $15 billion US ($4.5 billion EU, $10.6 billion non EU).

The number of national and international designers using fur has been steadily growing. Currently, more than 500 designers use fur worldwide.

Fur is produced humanely and in accordance with international, national and regional welfare laws and regulations. In Europe, which produces two thirds of the world's farmed fur, the fur farming sector is governed and abides by European animal welfare law as well as the Council of Europe standards. In addition to that the fur sector itself invests in animal welfare research on an ongoing basis.

Fur farming plays a valuable role in the recycling chain by making efficient use of the animal by-products of the fish and poultry industries. Each year over one million tonnes of these by-products are used in the EU alone.

Wild fur accounts for 15%–20% of the total amount of fur sold globally, with Canada, Russia and USA as main suppliers. The trade has supported research now formalised by international agreement to ensure that harvesting methods meet the highest animal welfare standards.

The majority of wild species used by the fur trade are taken as part of wildlife management programmes, necessary for the maintenance of biodiversity, healthy eco-systems, population and disease control. The wild species taken are abundant.

'Fur is produced humanely and in accordance with international, national and regional welfare laws'

The British Fur Trade Association is a member of the International Fur Trade Federation (IFTF). IFTF has supported the Convention of International Trade in Endangered Species since its inception in the 1970s and has been a full voting member of the International Union for Conservation of Nature (IUCN) for over 25 years. The fur trade condemns any cruelty to animals.

Origin assured

Origin Assured (OA™) is a new fur industry initiative that gives consumers and buyers an assurance about the provenance of the fur they are buying. When consumers see the OA™ label they can be certain that, wild or farmed, the fur comes from a country where national or local regulations or standards governing fur production are in force. For further information see www.originassured.com.

The fur trade accepts the right of animal rights organisations to hold their beliefs that humans should not use animals for any reason including for fur, leather, meat or dairy consumption or as pets. However, the fur trade also supports consumers' freedom of choice to buy or wear animal products.

'Stylish furs are now a key element in fashion more than ever'

The furrier's art

Fur garments are made up by furriers, skilled craftsmen and women, working in small workshops using remarkable skills which they have acquired over many years.

The furrier craftsmen study traditional and modern techniques in order to fashion fur – the soft versatile material with which designers love to work and women adore to wear. Fur embodies the traditions of human craftsmanship that few other modern products possess. However, fur is no longer confined to exclusive or expensive clothing or to full fur garments. It is also being used as trims and accessories.

'Fur farming plays a valuable role in the recycling chain, making efficient use of the animal by-products'

New and improved processing techniques have been developed, for use in preparing fur garments. These include plucking, shearing, knitting and weaving. This means that fur garments can be made more lightweight.

Why real fur?

Real fur cannot be matched for its beauty, softness and glamour. The attraction of real fur is also in its touch, its feel, and in its three-dimensional quality. Designers speak of the way real fur plays with light and movement.

Furthermore, real fur is a natural sustainable product, delivering rare benefits in sustaining fragile habitats and communities. This contrasts with most 'fake' fur which is manufactured from non-renewable petroleum-based products.

Real fur is a durable material – quite the opposite of disposable fashion. Provided it is well looked after, real fur will continue to look good for many years. Real fur can be re-styled into different pieces as fashion changes.

⇨ The above information is reprinted with kind permission from British Fur Trade. Please visit www.britishfur.co.uk for further information.

Dolphins are 'people' say scientists

Dolphins deserve to be treated as non-human 'persons' whose rights to life and liberty should be respected, scientists meeting in Canada have been told.

By John von Radowitz

A small group of experts in philosophy, conservation and dolphin behaviour were canvassing support for a 'Declaration of Rights for Cetaceans'.

They believe dolphins – and their whale cousins – are sufficiently intelligent and self-aware to justify the same ethical considerations given to humans.

Recognising cetaceans' rights would mean an end to whaling and the captivity of dolphins and whales, or their use in entertainment.

The move is based on years of research that has shown dolphins and whales to have large, complex brains and a human-like level of self-awareness.

This has led the experts to conclude that although non-human, dolphins and whales are 'people' in a philosophical sense, which has far-reaching implications.

Ethics expert Professor Tom White, from Loyola Marymount University, Los Angeles, author of *In Defence of Dolphins: The New Moral Frontier*, said: 'Dolphins are non-human persons. A person needs to be an individual. If individuals count, then the deliberate killing of individuals of this sort is ethically the equivalent of deliberately killing a human being.

'The captivity of beings of this sort, particularly in conditions that would not allow for a decent life, is ethically unacceptable; commercial whaling is ethically unacceptable.

'We're saying the science has shown that individuality, consciousness, self-awareness, is no longer a unique human property. That poses all kinds of challenges.'

The declaration, originally agreed in May 2010, contains the statements 'every individual cetacean has the right to life', 'no cetacean should be held in captivity or servitude, be subject to cruel treatment, or be removed from their natural environment', and 'no cetacean is the property of any state, corporation, human group or individual'.

It adds: 'The rights, freedoms and norms set forth in this declaration should be protected under international and domestic law.'

The US authors brought their message to the annual meeting of the American Association for the Advancement of Science (AAAS) in Vancouver, Canada, the world's biggest science conference.

Psychologist Dr Lori Marino, from Emory University in Atlanta, told how scientific advances had changed the view of the cetacean brain.

She said: 'We went from seeing the dolphin/whale brain as being a giant amorphous blob that doesn't carry a lot of intelligence and complexity to not only being an enormous brain but an enormous brain with an enormous amount of complexity, and a complexity that rivals our own. It's different in the way it's put together but in terms of the level of complexity it's very similar to the human brain.'

Dolphins had a sense of self which could be tested by the way they recognise themselves in mirrors, she added.

'When you get up in the morning and look in the mirror and know that's you, you have a sense of "you",' said Dr Marino. 'They have a similar sense. They can look in a mirror and say, "Hey, that's me".'

She argued that whaling was an example of mass murder rather than a commercial operation.

'Once you shift from seeing a being as a property, a commodity, a resource, to a person, an autonomous entity that has a right to life on his or her own terms, the whole framework shifts ... this is not about harvesting resources, this is about murder,' said Dr Marino.

The experts cited unusual examples of dolphin and whale behaviour both in the wild and in captivity:

⇨ A member of a group of orcas, or killer whales, in Patagonia had a damaged jaw and could not feed. The elderly whale was fed and kept alive by its companions.

⇨ Dolphins taking part in an experiment had to press one of two levers to distinguish between sounds, some of which were very similar. By pressing a third lever, they were able to tell the researchers they wanted to 'pass' on a particular test because it was too hard. 'When you place dolphins in a situation like that they respond in exactly the same way humans do,' said Dr Lori. 'They are accessing their own minds and thinking their own thoughts.'

⇨ A number of captive dolphins were rewarded with fish in return for tidying up their tank. One of them ripped up a large paper bag, hid away the pieces, and presented them one at a time to get multiple rewards.

⇨ In Iceland, killer whales and fishermen have been known to work together. The whales show the fishermen where to lay their nets, and in return are allowed to feed on part of the catch. Then they lead the fleet to the next fishing ground.

21 February 2012

⇨ Information from *The Belfast Telegraph*. Please visit www.belfasttelegraph.co.uk

PETA slavery case against SeaWorld dismissed, as whales are not people

Do animals have the same constitutional rights as humans? According to a US federal judge, they most certainly do not.

By Mandy Adwell

After People for the Ethical Treatment of Animals (PETA) launched a lawsuit against SeaWorld, accusing them of violating the 13th Amendment, which abolished slavery, judge Jeffrey Miller threw it out. The judge ruled that orcas do not have the same constitutional rights as people.

'Is PETA helping or hurting the cause by taking such extreme measures?'

The lawsuit was filed in the US district court of San Diego, with five of SeaWorld's performing orcas listed as plaintiffs: Katina, Tilikum, Corky, Kasatka and Ulises.

In his ruling, judge Jeffrey Miller wrote: 'The only reasonable interpretation of the 13th amendment's plain language is that it applies to persons and not to non-persons such as orcas.'

David Steinberg, a law professor at the Thomas Jefferson School of Law in San Diego, said the lawsuit is 'demeaning to the integrity and humanity of people who were owned as slaves'.

That's actually a pretty good point, and while I think it's ridiculous that animals are still held in captivity for our entertainment and forced out of their natural habitats to dance around in a tiny pool, putting whales on court documents as plaintiffs is equally ridiculous.

'Would you like to see places like SeaWorld not keep whales in captivity?'

I wouldn't mind taking out a court case against people who are so boring they find entertainment in a whale jumping out of water over and over, but that's neither here nor there.

2 September 2012

⇨ The above information is reprinted with kind permission from The9Billion. Please visit www.the9billion.com for further information.

Seals and sealing

Information from the International Fur Trade Federation.

Sealing around the world

Sealing is important to the people of coastal communities throughout the world. People in Australia, Canada, Estonia, Finland, Latvia, Lithuania, Greenland, Iceland, Namibia, Norway, Russia, Sweden, United Kingdom and the United States all hunt seals.

Conservation

The International Union for Conservation of Nature (IUCN), the largest and most respected conservation organisation in the world, supports the sustainable use of seals and other wildlife, as long as this is from abundant populations.

North Atlantic Harp seal populations increased from 1.8 million in the 1980s to 5.4 to 5.8 million today – a three-fold increase.

Seal hunting is undertaken as a managed hunt or cull in many parts of the world. As such, regulations as to how seals can be hunted, who can hunt them, and how many are taken are applied. Each adult seal eats from one to 1.4 metric tonnes of fish, annually. Maintaining a healthy balance of the marine ecosystem is a challenge with increased seal populations and declining fish populations. Without such sustainable harvest, animal herds are regulated by starvation and disease, which involves considerably more suffering than a well-controlled harvest.

'The sealskin vest I am wearing is the result of Inuit carrying out their economy and livelihood. By doing this sustainably, we are setting a positive example to the world'

Sheila Watt-Cloutier, President, Inuit Circumpolar Conference

Animal welfare

Wherever animals are being hunted or killed, be it in an abattoir, on a farm or in the wild, the quickest and least painful mode of killing must always be used.

Sealers are trained to work rapidly using methods that are regulated by government authorities. The North Atlantic harp seal hunt, in Canada and Greenland, is the largest in the world, where over 85% of seals killed in Canada are done so by firearm.

Both the Canadian Veterinary Medical Association and the Independent Veterinary Working Group have recognised that the rifle and the hakapik (club) are both appropriate tools in the humane hunt of seals. In Canada, hunting regulations are enforced by Department of Fisheries and Oceans staff and the Royal Canadian Mounted Police.

People and seals

Inuit

Despite exemptions for Inuit-hunted seal pelts, Inuit and Greenlandic communities were hardest hit by the 1983 seal import ban imposed by the European Economic Community and the resulting global collapse in seal prices. Losing one of their only economic options, these communities suffered enormous socioeconomic disintegration.

Coastal fishermen

Sealing by coastal fishermen has taken place for millennia, with commercial sealing by Europeans starting over 300 years ago. Today, all sealers are licensed and hunt from their own small fishing boats, as large vessels are prohibited for seal hunting.

To people living in isolated villages with a limited range of employment options, a few thousand dollars is significant. Considered in context, sealing can make an enormous impact on a family's well-being: seals provide a livelihood, but they also provide meat for the kitchen table. In Newfoundland and Labrador, it is estimated that the edible portion of one Harp seal is worth an equivalent of $150 of store-bought meat. In the Arctic, where store-bought food is very expensive, the value of the edible meat of a single ringed seal is well over $200.

Products of the seal harvest

Approximately 15,000 people in the North Atlantic derive some income from sealing, in the way of meat, oils and pelts. Seal meat is very rich in protein, calcium, iron, magnesium and vitamin B-12.

Omega-3 supplements are known to be helpful in preventing and treating diabetes, arthritis, epilepsy and cardiovascular disease – the leading cause of death in industrialised countries.

The skins of seals are extremely valuable for clothing. They are full of oil, increasing their water repellence, yet they are also porous, which allows body humidity to escape. These characteristics make seal skin very useful for winter coats, hats or boots.

⇨ Information from the International Fur Trade Federation. Please visit www.wearefur.com

© *International Fur Trade Federation*

Why commercial sealing is cruel

It is hard to portray just how cruel the business of commercial sealing is. The need to prioritise speed and profit, combined with an unpredictable environment makes it virtually impossible to ensure humane killing.

Seal hunting in Canada

Each spring off the East Coast of Canada, hunters take their boats into dangerous waters or rush across moving ice pans in attempts to kill as many baby seals as possible in the short time available. Seal pups, most too young to escape, are either shot or hit with a spiked wooden club called a hakapik.

Although the Canadian Government compares the commercial seal hunt to the killing of farm animals, they have little in common. Unlike abattoirs, the commercial slaughter of seals takes place in an unpredictable, unmanageable environment where humane killing is impossible to achieve consistently.

IFAW believes Canada's commercial seal hunt can never be made acceptably humane. Here's why:

1. Competitive, commercial pressures make speed more important than humane killing.

The seal hunt is effectively a race between sealers to collect as many skins as possible before the quota is reached. Sometimes as many as 150,000 seals have been killed in two days. Under such conditions, humane killing isn't a priority and is rarely achieved.

2. Seal hunting involves unacceptably high wounding rates.

When rifles are shot from moving boats at escaping seals or when the animals are chased across the ice pans with hunters swinging their hakapiks, it is unlikely a seal will be stunned effectively with a single blow or shot. Instead, animals are left wounded and terrified, lingering on the ice in pain, suffering and distress. Some seals are struck and lost.

3. The current Marine Mammal Regulations do not set out requirements for humane killing of seals.

Sanctioned hunting practices permit the most inhumane activities: live and conscious animals are impaled on steel hooks; seals can be shot at from moving boats and in open water; multiple animals can be shot before testing for unconsciousness, wounded seals may be left to suffer; and bleeding out is not required immediately after checking for unconsciousness. The requirements for humane slaughter are neither legislated nor practised.

4. Effective monitoring and enforcement is impossible.

Our over 40 years of seal hunt observation indicate that any regulations are impossible to enforce. Boats are widely dispersed over hundreds of thousands of square kilometres, and hundreds, sometimes thousands, of boats take part. With only a few vessels available to enforce the hunt, officials face an impossible task.

5. Endemic disregard for the Regulations indicates the Department of Fisheries and Oceans is unwilling – and unable – to enforce any rules that might be in place.

There is a clear conflict of interest in having the Department of Fisheries and Oceans responsible for enforcing the Regulations and at the same time defending the 'humaneness' of the seal hunt.

The evidence gathered by IFAW demonstrates that Canada's commercial seal hunt is not conducted humanely and that monitoring and enforcement is all but impossible. Commerical sealing is inherently inhumane and seals – like all wild animals – should not be exploited for commercial gain.

⇨ Reprinted with permission of IFAW – the International Fund for Animal Welfare, www.ifaw.org.

© International Fund for Animal Welfare 2012

If you really care about animals, please don't visit zoos...

Information from Merseyside Animal Rights.

Every bank holiday weekend the queues at zoos and aquaria are huge. Everyone wants a glimpse of the exotic animals and cute babies. What most zoo patrons don't stop to consider is that although they are likely to be in the zoo for a couple of hours, the animals never get to leave. Many visitors will spend less than three minutes looking at most exhibits and some get looked at for less than eight seconds.

'Many visitors will spend less than three minutes looking at most exhibits'

Even the 'best' zoos cannot give animals the space which they would live in, in the wild. If they did, the visitors would never be able to see the 'exhibits', besides no zoo could afford to own land large enough to give large mammals their natural range. The vast majority of animals in zoos are not from the UK, so their natural habitat is different to the one here. To meet the animals' needs would require artificial heating or cooling; the humidity may need to be increased or decreased; plants and ecosystems the animals depend on would also have to be simulated. Most zoos fail badly in attempts to create these conditions, leaving arctic animals with only painted scenes of the tundra they have been snatched from and desert creatures sheltering from British winter snow.

The animals in zoos are so stressed and removed from their natural situations that they act oddly. Many become reclusive, attempting to hide from the preying eyes of the public in their tiny enclosures. Others exhibit stereotypic behaviours, such as excessively grooming themselves or pacing restlessly up against the bars of their cages. Some become aggressive and others will self-harm. Some zoos put on performances using their animals, similar to the ways in which circuses do. The animals are required to perform degrading tricks which when repeated twice daily can damage their sensitive bodies.

Population control, in both the form of increasing the number of animals on display and providing cute babies to draw in the public and reducing numbers to prevent over crowding compromises animal welfare. Artificial insemination may be used, or inadequate pairing based on the zoos' preferences not the animals' may result in fighting between animals. Often the stressful situations into which baby animals are born causes mothers to abandon or even kill their own offspring as the situation is unfavourable to their surroundings.

Case study

The high profile case of the polar bear Knut highlights the issues. Knut and his brother were born to an ex-circus polar bear. The babies were abandoned by their mother in a German zoo and she may have killed them if the zoo keepers had not intervened. The second cub died after four days with an infection. Knut was the first polar bear in the zoo to survive beyond infancy in over 30 years; he had to be raised by human handlers. As the bear has grown less cuddly the numbers of visitors coming to see him have decreased. As he is used to large amounts of human attention he becomes upset when he doesn't have an audience to play to. It is likely that the zoo will try and use him to father other bears in order to once again attract the large crowds that Knut did in his first months.

'Being in zoos negatively affects animals' emotional well-being'

The situation with this polar bear shows how zoos want young animals to attract the crowds, yet the mothers abandon their young because the environment isn't what they need to thrive. It also shows how being in zoos negatively affects animals' emotional well-being as they become dependent on humans for everything. It also highlights the links between zoos and circuses.

Often when there is an abundance of a species the zoo will sell on 'excess' animals to circuses or for meat. There has recently been

controversy about the zoo which Knut is in, as there have been allegations that the zoo has sold a pygmy hippopotamus and a family of Asiatic black bears for slaughter in two separate deals conducted in the early 1990s. During the foot and mouth crisis, zoos were found to be feeding some of their exhibits to the animals which pull greater crowds, showing how much zoo managers really care for their charges.

Often zoos keep just one or two examples of a species to show visitors. These animals are often species which live in large herds and can only function properly in such an environment. Other zoos, or even enclosures in the same zoos, house far too many of one species in a small space, resulting in aggression and bullying of weaker animals, sometimes resulting in their death.

Zoos try to argue against their critics by saying that they work on conservation projects to improve the habitats for animals in the wild. They are legally obligated to engage in conservation work, the scale of which depends on the size of the zoo. Some small animal collections are required to merely maintain hedges and ponds on their site to satisfy their legal obligations. Other larger zoos may engage in breeding programmes or donate money to groups protecting wild areas. While some zoos do breed endangered animals, there is rarely any system for returning these animals to the wild. Those which do have had to have reintroduction schemes halted indefinitely when they find the animals are not able to fend for themselves. There have been cases where just before animals were to be released they were found to be harbouring diseases which could have wiped out the remains of the wild population. The answer to saving wild species is not to keep a small number forever imprisoned in zoos, or to try and breed animals in captivity, but to protect their habitat from damage, prevent poaching and stop wild animals being caught and put into zoos, as sadly is still on going. Captive Animal Protection Society (CAPS), found that 79%

of all animals in British aquaria, marine zoos, are wild caught! It has been estimated that it costs 50 times more to keep an elephant in a breeding programme in a zoo than it would to protect the habitat needed to sustain the animal in the wild. Pretending that money paid to zoos helps animals is a farce.

'The animals which are seen in zoos are prisoners who can teach us nothing about their wild cousins'

Another common zoo argument is that zoos educate members of the public who would never otherwise see these animals, and that this education can lead to future protection of the species. Sadly the animals which are seen in zoos are bored, humiliated, enclosed prisoners who can teach us nothing about their wild cousins who have to rely on their own intelligence and resources to survive in the wild. This argument is no longer valid, now that we have TV documentaries and websites which inform us about how animals exist naturally in other places. We would be better off taking our children into the countryside around us and showing them the last wild species here and teaching them about British habitat protection and respect for life.

'The animals in zoos are so stressed and removed from their natural situations that they act oddly'

If you really care about animals please don't visit zoos. Paying to see these animals simply funds the abuse of more animals.

⇨ Information reprinted with kind permission from Merseyside Animal Rights. Please visit www.merseysideanimalrights. co.uk for further information on this and other subjects.

© Merseyside Animal Rights

Zoos and aquariums save the world's most endangered species

At the occasion of the World Environment Day WAZA publishes a press release on the role of zoos and aquariums in species conservation.

Gland, Switzerland, Thursday 2 June 2011, (WAZA): 'The role of zoos and aquariums is often misunderstood as being only entertainment menageries; however, they actually play a vital role in species conservation,' says Dr Gerald Dick, Executive Director of the World Association of Zoos and Aquariums (WAZA).

Apart from field conservation and environmental education work, many zoos have taken on the additional role of breeding a growing number of species that only exist in those facilities.

29 of the 34 animal species currently classified as Extinct in the Wild are actively bred in zoos, aquariums and other animal propagation facilities.

Several species that are extinct in the wild due to habitat destruction, poaching, wildlife trade or climate change are now solely represented by animals in zoos and aquariums.

At the occasion of the World Environment Day, on 5 June 2011, WAZA wants to emphasise the crucial role played by zoos and aquariums in species conservation around the world.

One important aspect of the work of zoos and aquariums is the establishment of viable populations of species that went extinct in the wild. Through coordinated breeding programmes, reintroduction projects are one important option for many of those species and zoos and aquariums help to bridge the gap. Conservation breeding programmes are in place for numerous species.

There are 34 animal species currently classified as Extinct in the Wild on the IUCN Red List of Threatened Species™ (see Appendices 1 and 2 of the list). 29 of these species are actively bred in zoos, aquariums and other animal propagation facilities. Recovery efforts using captive-bred animals are being implemented for 22 species (65%) classified as Extinct in the Wild.

A recent evaluation of the impact of conservation on the status of the world's vertebrates, published in the journal *Science*, showed that conservation breeding in zoos and aquariums played a role in the recovery of 19 of the 68 species (28%) whose threat status was reduced according to the IUCN Red List. In this evaluation, species previously classified as Extinct in the Wild that have improved in status thanks to the reintroduction of captive-bred animals include the Przewalski's horse (*Equus ferus przewalskii*), black-footed ferret (*Mustela nigripes*) and California condor (*Gymnogyps californianus*).

'On average, 52 species of mammals, birds and amphibians move closer to extinction each year. If it was not for the breeding efforts in zoological institutions, the rate of deterioration would be even worse,' says Dr Markus Gusset, Conservation Officer & International Studbook Coordinator of WAZA.

The Takhi also called the Przewalski's horse is one of the flagship species of zoo-related conservation success.

It is the only living representative of wild horses, which ranged from Germany and the Russian steppes east to Kazakhstan, Mongolia and northern China until the late 18th century. After this time, the species went into catastrophic decline and the last confirmed sighting in the wild was made in 1969. Under the aegis of WAZA, an international studbook forms the backbone of a global conservation breeding programme, containing records of animals as far back as 1899. Several WAZA member institutions keep takhi, including Smithsonian National Zoological Park, Zoos South Australia and Prague Zoo. Following the successful reintroduction of captive-bred animals in Mongolia and elsewhere since the 1990s, takhi once again range freely in the wild. The International Takhi Group, whose conservation project for the takhi has been endorsed and supported by WAZA, is one of the organisations strongly involved in the conservation of this species.

6 January 2011

⇨ The above information is reprinted with kind permission from the World Association of Zoos and Aquariums. Please visit www.waza.org for further information.

Horse fighting

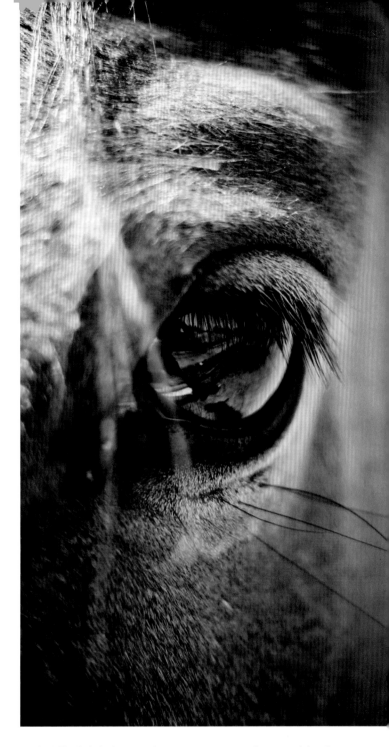

Horse fighting occurs throughout the island of Mindanao in the southern Philippines during fiestas. Billed as a cultural tradition specific to indigenous communities, it is prominent enough to warrant local television coverage, municipal support in the form of cash prizes and sponsorship from local businesses.

Background

While horse fighting is promoted under the guise of tradition, in reality, extensive gambling on the outcomes of the horse fights, with bets running as high as £2,000, is the main reason it has become so prevalent. Currently, thousands of horses are involved in hundreds of fights throughout the southern Philippines, with some fiestas organising up to 20 fights per day over a three-day period.

Current legislation

Republic Act 8485, also known as the Animal Welfare Act, outlawed all horse fighting in 1998. However, with penalties ranging from a minimum of 1,000 pesos (approx. £10) to a maximum of 5,000 pesos (approx. £50) horse-fighting organisers pay little heed to the law, and the events take place in broad daylight in public areas.

Lack of enforcement

Despite being illegal, not one person has been prosecuted for engaging in horse fighting since the passage of RA 8485 in 1998. Modest attempts to curtail horse fighting have been instituted by the national government's Animal Welfare Division, to no avail. Local government in the regions where horse fighting is prevalent is fiercely protective of the activity and generally defies the national government's authority on the issue. Often, local police are even hired by the promoters for crowd control purposes.

Animal welfare violations

Horse fighting is a spectator blood sport where two stallions (male horses), are incited to fight each other in a controlled environment over a mare (female horse) in heat. Events are conducted in city stadiums or large fenced in areas before raucous crowds who attend in anticipation of intense fighting, gore and even death. With high stakes in the balance, most horse fights involve purpose-bred and trained animals who are large, sturdy and aggressive. The training process is brutal, involving fights with other horses, which handlers control by tying long ropes around the horse's necks, and pulling heavy sleds up hills to build strength.

During a typical horse fight two stallions are presented to a mare in heat, who remains in the ring during the fight. The stallions bite, kick and strike each other with their hooves, inflicting serious injuries until one of them submits, flees or is killed. Injuries such as gouges, gashes and broken limbs sustained during fights are always serious and can be fatal. Veterinary observers report seeing horses being struck with such force to the head that their eyes literally pop out of their sockets, horses having their entire ears torn off during fights, and horses drenched in blood from their injuries. While most fights last about 15 minutes, many can go on for up to three hours. In one reported instance, a fight lasted six hours, ending only because one of the horses was so badly injured and exhausted, he was no longer able to stand up.

⇨ The above information is reprinted with kind permission from Network for Animals. Please visit www.networkforanimals.org for further information.

Animal research: fast facts

Information from Understanding Animal Research.

Why are animals used in research?

Four main reasons:

⇨ To advance scientific understanding

⇨ As models to study disease

⇨ To develop and test new medical treatments

⇨ To protect the safety of people, animals and the environment.

Animals are needed to find out what happens in the whole, living body, which is far more complex than the sum of its parts.

Most major medical advances have depended in part on the use of animals in research.

Are there alternatives?

Most biological and medical research uses non-animal methods. While these are sometimes regarded as alternatives, they are normally used alongside animals to answer different research questions.

How is animal research regulated?

The law requires animals are only used when the information cannot be obtained in another way, and the results will be sufficiently important to justify the use of animals.

The UK is the only country in the world to have both local and national controls running at the same time.

The Home Office is responsible for the regulation of animal experiments in the UK and the independent Animal Procedures Committee is a body that advises the Home Secretary.

Three separate licences are required for animal procedures. Researchers adhere to ethical, scientific and legal guidelines, requiring that laboratory animals are treated well and used in minimum numbers.

Inspectors from the Home Office, all qualified vets and doctors, make regular visits to all animal facilities, usually without warning.

Recently, the European Directive which governs the use of animals in research was revised, and this legislation is currently being transposed into UK law.

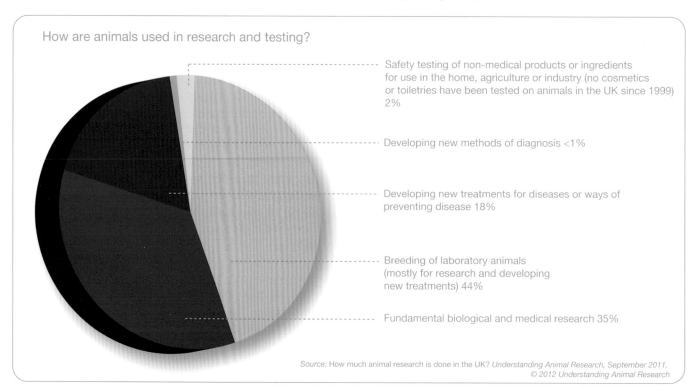

How are animals used in research and testing?

Safety testing of non-medical products or ingredients for use in the home, agriculture or industry (no cosmetics or toiletries have been tested on animals in the UK since 1999) 2%

Developing new methods of diagnosis <1%

Developing new treatments for diseases or ways of preventing disease 18%

Breeding of laboratory animals (mostly for research and developing new treatments) 44%

Fundamental biological and medical research 35%

Source: How much animal research is done in the UK? Understanding Animal Research, September 2011.
© 2012 Understanding Animal Research

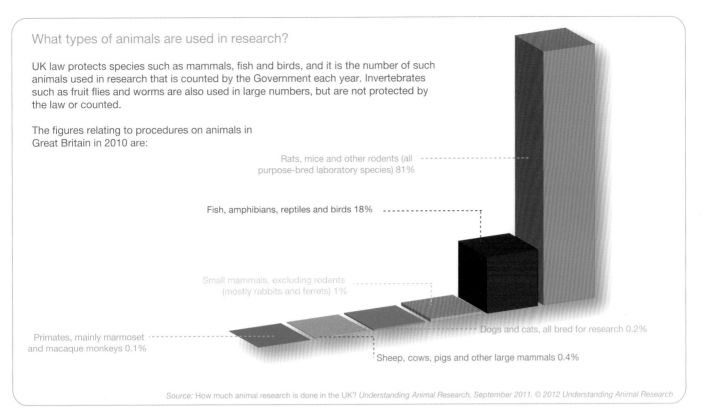

What types of animals are used in research?

UK law protects species such as mammals, fish and birds, and it is the number of such animals used in research that is counted by the Government each year. Invertebrates such as fruit flies and worms are also used in large numbers, but are not protected by the law or counted.

The figures relating to procedures on animals in Great Britain in 2010 are:

Rats, mice and other rodents (all purpose-bred laboratory species) 81%

Fish, amphibians, reptiles and birds 18%

Small mammals, excluding rodents (mostly rabbits and ferrets) 1%

Primates, mainly marmoset and macaque monkeys 0.1%

Dogs and cats, all bred for research 0.2%

Sheep, cows, pigs and other large mammals 0.4%

Source: How much animal research is done in the UK? *Understanding Animal Research, September 2011. © 2012 Understanding Animal Research*

How many animals and what type of animals are used?

In 2010, 3.72 million animals were used in scientific procedures in the UK. This does not include invertebrates such as fruit flies or worms, or animals which are killed only for their tissue. Most of the animals used are rodents or fish.

Cats, dogs and primates such as macaques and marmosets make up less than 0.5% of the animals used. Great apes have not been used in the UK for over 25 years.

Opinions and ethical stances

Polls consistently show that around three-quarters of the UK public agree that animal research is necessary to advance medicine.

All major scientific and medical organisations around the world agree that animal research is crucial for our understanding of the body in health and disease and for the development and testing of new medical treatments.

Anti-vivisection groups and animal rights extremists share an ideological opposition to any use of animals in research, but use different tactics.

Animal rights extremists use criminal tactics to frighten researchers into stopping their work. Most of the extremists in the UK have now been jailed for their campaigns of harassment and intimidation.

⇨ Information from Understanding Animal Research. Visit www. understanginganimalresearch. org.uk for further information.

© 2012 Understanding Animal Research

Myths and facts

Understanding Animal Research lists more than 20 common misconceptions about animal research and provide some facts to help you make up your mind on where you stand.

Research on animals is not relevant to people because animals are different from people.

All mammals are descended from common ancestors, so humans are biologically very similar to other mammals. All mammals, including humans, have the same organs – heart, lungs, kidneys, liver, etc. – that work in the same way, controlled via the bloodstream and nervous system.

Of course there are minor differences, but these are far outweighed by the remarkable similarities. The differences can also give important clues about diseases and how they might be treated – for instance, if we knew why the mouse with muscular dystrophy suffers less muscle wasting than human patients, this might lead to a treatment for this debilitating and fatal disorder.

Vitamins work in the same way in animals as they do in people – research on guinea pigs led to the discovery of how vitamin C works. Hormones found in animals also work in a similar way in people. The following animal hormones have all been used successfully in human patients: insulin from pigs or cows; thyrotropin from cows; calcitonin from salmon; adrenocorticotrophic hormone from farm animals; oxytocin and vasopressin from pigs.

Animal research on animals is not relevant because people and animals suffer from different illnesses.

In fact many veterinary medicines are the same as those used for human patients: examples include antibiotics, pain killers and tranquillisers. Many of the veterinary medicines that are used to treat animals are the same as, or very similar to, those used to treat human patients.

Most human diseases exist in at least one other species. Many different animals naturally get illnesses such as cancer, heart failure, asthma, rabies and malaria and they can be treated in much the same way as human patients. There is evidence that dinosaurs suffered from arthritis. Chimpanzees can get polio and the human vaccine has been used to protect them in the wild.

Animal testing doesn't work and causes drug side-effects

Medicines are only tested on animals after extensive screening by computer and test-tube methods. Animal tests show how the medicine reacts in the living body and detect toxic effects before it is given to human volunteers.

Problems that will not be revealed by test-tube results will often show up in animal tests. For instance, a medicine given by mouth may be altered by digestion, becoming less effective or more toxic. The animal tests aim to reveal major undesirable effects such as liver damage, raised blood pressure, nerve damage, or damage to the fetus. The results will give a strong indication of what the effects in people are likely to be. It is obviously important, and is required by law, to find out about potential problems before medicines are given to human volunteers and patients in clinical trials.

The new medicine will be tested on around 15 times as many human volunteers as animals. Human clinical trials will involve testing a potential drug on 3–5,000 human volunteers and patients. If a side-effect (affecting say one in 10,000 patients) shows up only after this stage, then it is difficult to see how it could have been spotted before.

Medicines that work in people are toxic to animals and vice versa.

A common myth is that penicillin is toxic to guinea pigs. It is only toxic at very high doses (a similar effect to long-term penicillin use in human patients). Like many other medicines, at equivalent doses to those used to treat people, it is not toxic.

Another common myth is that thalidomide didn't cause birth defects in animals. In fact it wasn't tested in pregnant animals before it was prescribed to pregnant women. As soon as the tragic effects on unborn babies came to light, testing of thalidomide on pregnant animals showed it had very similar effects in many species. This led directly to the introduction of the UK Medicines Act in 1968.

There is an endless list of drugs that have to be withdrawn because of side effects and these side-effects are a major cause of hospital deaths.

Only around four in every 100 medicines are withdrawn after their launch because of side-effects which were undetected during both human and animal tests.

Of the 2,000 types of medicine on the market, since 1961 only about 40 have been withdrawn in the UK, US, France or Germany due to serious side-effects. This indicates a success rate of at least 98% for medicines testing. Only ten of the 40 medicines withdrawn have been withdrawn in all four countries.

Numbers of drug-induced deaths or hospitalisation due to side-effects are often exaggerated or misleading. Most of these deaths are not caused by normal doses of drugs, but are in fact due to accidental or deliberate overdose.

The side-effects and subsequent withdrawal of the arthritis treatment Vioxx were due to animal tests.

Vioxx was extensively studied in thousands of human patients, both before and after it was approved by

The making of a medicine

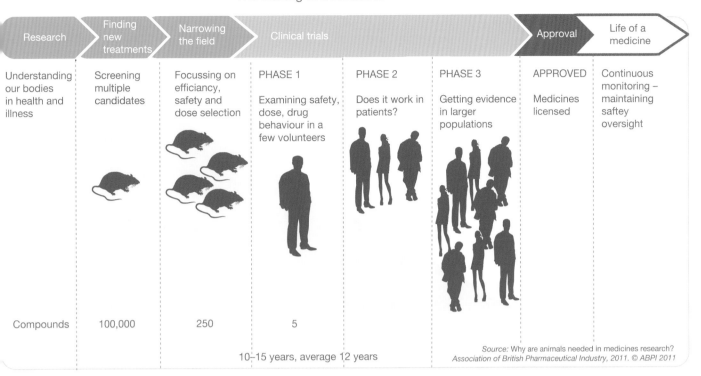

Research	Finding new treatments	Narrowing the field	Clinical trials			Approval	Life of a medicine
Understanding our bodies in health and illness	Screening multiple candidates	Focussing on efficiancy, safety and dose selection	**PHASE 1** Examining safety, dose, drug behaviour in a few volunteers	**PHASE 2** Does it work in patients?	**PHASE 3** Getting evidence in larger populations	**APPROVED** Medicines licensed	Continuous monitoring – maintaining saftey oversight
Compounds	100,000	250	5				

10–15 years, average 12 years

Source: Why are animals needed in medicines research? *Association of British Pharmaceutical Industry, 2011. © ABPI 2011*

over 70 regulatory agencies around the world. For any new medicine, animal and other tests are meant to help work out if the medicine is safe enough for human trials. In the case of Vioxx, the answer was yes – animal tests did their job well.

Only when over 80 million patients around the world had taken this medicine and some long-term patient studies had been conducted was the increased risk of heart attack firmly established.

One answer to the problem of rare drug side-effects is better scrutiny after approval. This would help to predict which patients might react badly – because of their genetic make-up, multiple illnesses or interactions with other medication.

Animal research doesn't work and hasn't made any contribution to medical progress.

The discovery of insulin in dogs in the 1920s by Banting and Best is a good example of the contribution of animal research to medical progress. Before the discovery of insulin, there was no effective treatment for the disease and people with diabetes usually died tragically young. Diabetic dogs have also benefited from insulin treatment.

Each decade since the discovery of insulin has seen the introduction of new kinds of treatments for many diseases. Each of these and many other advances were critically dependent on animal research.

Given continued research using animals, we can expect further advances in the treatment of diseases such as Alzheimer's disease, cancer, cystic fibrosis and crippling joint disease. It is very difficult to see how we could make such medical advances without animal research.

Four independent reports have found that animal studies make an important contribution to scientific and medical advances.

The clinical trial tragedy (testing the medicine TGN1412) at Northwick Park shows that animal tests don't work.

TGN1412 is one of the newer 'biological' medicines. None of the tests carried out before the clinical trial predicted its tragic side-effects. The expert inquiry described the human blood cell tests as a 'striking failure', and the clinical trial itself was poorly designed. Testing the safety and effectiveness of such treatments is more difficult than most medicines, but many biologicals which have been developed in animals, like Herceptin, are already saving lives.

There are around 300 clinical trials every year in the UK. Yet the kind of problem seen at Northwick Park Hospital is very rare, partly because animal and other tests are so good at discovering problems. To suggest that we abandon some tests because they are not 100% perfect is like saying that we should stop wearing seat belts because they do not prevent all injuries.

25 years of primate research has failed to find vaccines, cures or treatments for AIDS.

HIV has been difficult to tackle because the virus fools the body's immune system. It is true that we do not yet have an effective vaccine. Some leading researchers are now suggesting that more basic research should be performed before trialling vaccines in patients – which does remain the ultimate goal of research.

However, animal studies were crucial in identifying the virus, for developing diagnostic tests, and for producing therapies such as antiretrovirals that have prolonged millions of lives. These medicines mean that HIV can be a manageable chronic condition rather than an automatic death sentence, as it was in the 1980s.

Systematic reviews demonstrate that animal studies are meaningless for human health.

Systematic reviews can help to tell us whether studies are being properly carried out and published. For example, a systematic review in the respected medical journal *The Lancet* showed that none of the 500 human clinical trials for an illness called tardive dyskinesia produced any useful data.

Systematic reviews have shown that all types of study can be improved. Where they have been carried out, systematic reviews and other independent studies have shown that animal studies can be relevant for human medical advances.

However, systematic reviews simply cannot provide all the answers. A lot depends on how studies are selected for review. For most animal research, the aim is not to predict what will happen in human trials, but to discover new knowledge or make advances in understanding diseases.

In many cases comparing the results of animal research and results from human trials is as meaningless as comparing apples and oranges.

Animals don't need to be used in research because there are alternatives.

We cannot yet reproduce complex diseases in a cell culture, get a computer to cough, or examine a whole beating heart in a test-tube. By law, animals must not be used in a research project if viable non-animal techniques are available.

Most research is already carried out using these other methods. But we still need to use animals at some point. The living body is much more than just a collection of its parts; we need to understand how they interact. Humans can only be used in limited situations.

Scientists have strong ethical, economic and legal obligations to use animals in research only when necessary. Thus the number of research animals used annually in the UK has almost halved in the last 30 years. As science progresses, it may be possible to reduce further the numbers of animals used in some areas. In other areas, the numbers of animals may increase.

The guiding principles in animal research today are called the three Rs: Refinement, to make sure animals suffer as little as possible; Reduction, to minimise the number of animals used; Replacement, to replace animals with non-animal techniques wherever possible.

Magnetic Resonance Imaging (MRI) can now be used on humans to get the same level of information as invasive brain studies in animals.

Functional MRI (fMRI) measures blood flow in different parts of the brain. It can be used in human volunteers without ill effect. But it does not give anything like the same level of detailed information that can be achieved by painlessly inserting electrodes into brain tissue in animal or human studies.

Microdosing can replace animal safety tests.

Microdosing is used to study how very small doses of potential medicines behave in human volunteers (sometimes called Phase 0 human trials). It should make the drug discovery process more efficient by highlighting earlier whether a compound is effective. New, urgently needed medicines could be available sooner and more cheaply as a result.

If microdosing shows that certain potential medicines are not suitable, it should reduce the number of animals used because these compounds would not need to be further developed and tested. But compounds that look promising would need to go through development and testing involving animals.

Microdosing has limitations like any other method of testing. There is no guarantee that the body's reaction to a microdose will be the same as it is to a full dose. It is a relatively new method and has yet to be fully validated, although it looks promising.

Vaccines and antibiotics have achieved nothing. Public health measures such as clean water and good sanitation are the solution to the problem of infectious disease.

Improvements such as clean water and good sanitation were responsible for a dramatic drop in the great water-borne infectious diseases of the nineteenth century. However, by the 1940s and 50s, when clean water and good sanitation were standard in the UK, there were still hundreds of thousands of cases of these often fatal diseases every year.

Vaccines have virtually eradicated some 'old' diseases like TB, diphtheria and cholera in developed countries. Recent vaccination programmes, such has meningitis and MMR, have greatly reduced childhood infections. When vaccination is not taken up by a good majority the number of cases, of measles for instance, rises.

Smallpox was eradicated thanks largely to a worldwide vaccination programme and the World Health Organization aims to eliminate polio worldwide by immunisation. Newer diseases such as HIV and many tropical diseases such as malaria will only be effectively tackled by vaccines.

Many pointless, unnecessary animal experiments are carried out.

Unnecessary animal experiments are very unlikely in the UK for the following reasons:

⇨ The strict controls on animal research, in the Animals (Scientific Procedures) Act 1986, do not allow animals to be used to obtain information that is obtainable by other means.

⇨ Research using animals is very expensive because the animals are costly to buy or breed, to house, and to care for, and the work itself is slow and labour intensive.

⇨ Funds for biomedical research are limited, so each research proposal is rigorously assessed by panels of experts. Irrelevant work will not gain funding.

Animal research is a cheap and easy option and is carried out for profit.

If researchers were motivated by the desire for profit, rather than the desire to establish scientific fact, then animal experimentation is the last technique they would adopt, since it is much more expensive than other, non-animal methods.

The high cost is largely due to the number of staff required to look after the animals' welfare. Vets are on call 24/7 and all animal technicians must have months of specific training to look after the animals.

Most research animals are cats, dogs or monkeys.

More than 80 out of every 100 animals used in research are mice, rats and other rodents. Only one in every 1,000 research animals is a cat or a dog.

Dogs, because of the size and similarity of their organs, are important for the development of new surgical techniques and for the study of the heart, lungs and blood vessels. Cats are important in the study of hearing and brain function. The use of both cats and dogs is subject to particular controls which require that they are specially bred for research. Stray cats and dogs or lost pets are not used for research in Britain.

Some people believe that monkeys and apes (primates) are used in great numbers, but monkeys represent less than one in every 2,000 research animals. Apes are not used at all in the UK and Europe. Smaller primates such as macaques and marmosets are needed for research into very serious conditions such as AIDS and Alzheimer's disease.

There are no laws or regulations protecting laboratory animals.

Around the world the welfare of animals in research is protected by national and international legislation, by local laws or by ethical committees. The UK is widely recognised as having the most comprehensive regulations covering laboratory animal welfare. Uniquely, UK researchers must both comply with stringent national regulations and submit their research proposals to local ethical review.

Researchers do not care about the well-being of laboratory animals.

Researchers are concerned about the welfare of the animals that they study and this concern is both humane and scientific. Scientists are at least as caring as other people and, like anyone else, often have pets of their own. They have no reason to mistreat research animals and good reason for treating them well, because the use of unhealthy, stressed or frightened animals would reduce the reliability of an experiment's results. Researchers make sure that their animals are well fed, well housed and kept free of infections and other illnesses.

Laboratory animals suffer great pain and distress.

Most animal research involves mild procedures such as taking a blood sample, giving a single injection, or having a change of diet. If more invasive procedures are necessary, then anaesthetics and pain relief will be given whenever appropriate.

It is in researchers' interests to make sure animals suffer as little as possible; stressed animals are less likely to produce reliable results. All animal research must pass an ethical evaluation which weighs up its pros and cons and decides whether it is justified. The research then has to be approved by Home Office Inspectors, who are all doctors or vets and who ensure that high welfare standards are applied.

Any animal suffering undue pain or distress that cannot be alleviated must be put down immediately and painlessly: this is the law.

Animals are used for testing cosmetics.

Testing of cosmetics and cosmetic ingredients on animals has been banned in the UK since 1998. A Europe-wide ban is scheduled to come into force in 2010.

⇨ Information from Understanding Animal Research. www.understandinganimalresearch.org.uk.

Ethical issues

Is it morally acceptable to cause pain, suffering and death to animals?

The question of defining the moral status of humans and animals often arises in the debate on research involving animals. Are humans morally more important than all animals? Is there a sliding scale with humans at the top and the simplest animals at the bottom? Or are humans and animals morally equal?

We suggest that the proper moral treatment of a being depends on the characteristics it possesses, rather than simply on the species to which it belongs. We identify five morally relevant features:

⇨ Sentience (the capacity to feel pleasure and pain)

⇨ Higher cognitive capacities (for example, the ability to use language and learn complicated tasks, such as making and using tools)

⇨ The capacity to flourish (the ability to satisfy species-specific needs)

⇨ Sociability (being a member of a community)

⇨ Possession of a life (attributing value to life itself).

Ethical decision making

What weight should be given to each of the morally relevant features in considering whether or not research is acceptable? Are they factors to be weighed against human benefit? Should they be understood as absolute constraints? For example, should any use of animals that are capable of suffering be prohibited, or only the use of those that have higher cognitive capacities?

Many people seem to support a 'hybrid' approach. This involves a combination of laying down definite limits for what should and should not happen (for example: 'animals with higher cognitive capacities, such as chimpanzees, should never be used in research') and weighing up the costs and benefits of a particular action (for example: 'research that causes minimum pain to a mouse is acceptable if it helps to ascertain the safety of an important and frequently used chemical').

This approach can also be found in the Animals (Scientific Procedures) Act 1986: the costs and benefits have to be weighed for each project and there are specific policies that prevent the use of the Great Apes and the use of animals in the testing of new cosmetics.

The ethical debate comes down to disagreement on two questions:

1. What are the definite limits?

2. How do we weigh the different morally relevant factors within the permitted limits?

To provide answers, we need to consider at least five further related questions:

⇨ What are the goals of research?

⇨ What is the probability of success?

⇨ Which animals are to be used?

⇨ What effect will there be on the animals used in the experiment?

⇨ Are there any alternatives?

Ethical positions

After considering these questions, members of the Working Party agreed that there was no single view to which they could all subscribe, thus reflecting the range of views that exists in society. Instead, we describe four possible ethical positions, which represent points on a continuum.

The report does not advocate any one viewpoint as 'right'. Rather, the reader is invited to decide which they find to be the most acceptable.

⇨ Information from the Nuffield Council on Bioethics. www.nuffieldbioethics.org.

The 'anything goes' view

If humans see value in research involving animals, then it requires no further ethical justification (no member of the Working Party took this position).

The 'on balance justification' view

Research involving animals is morally acceptable if the costs are outweighed by the benefits, but every reasonable step must be taken to reduce the harm to animals.

The 'moral dilemma' view

Most forms of research involving animals pose moral dilemmas. Animal research is morally unacceptable, but so is avoiding research that could be beneficial to humans or animals.

The 'abolitionist' view

There is no moral justification for any harmful research on animals that is not to the benefit of the individual animal. Humans experiment on animals not because it is right but because they can.

Victims of charity…

A report on the cruel and scientifically invalid experiments funded by medical research charities.

By Andrew Tyler, Director, Animal Aid

The medical research charities that are the focus of this report are well-regarded British institutions, charged with seeking remedies for health problems that devastate millions of lives every year. As well as laboratory research, they devote a proportion of their income to providing practical support for affected patients and their families.

Animal Aid's interest in Cancer Research UK, the British Heart Foundation, Parkinson's UK and the Alzheimer's Society relates to the animal experiments they fund. The appalling suffering meted out in the course of such experiments – to mice, monkeys, goats, pigs, dogs and other animals – is sufficient reason for them to be stopped. Animals' brains are deliberately damaged with toxic chemicals, or their hearts are slowly and systematically destroyed. Animals are tormented in water mazes, injected with cancerous tissue and subjected to breeding programmes that produce weakened, disease-prone, mentally deranged 'mutants'. The agonies they endure are described – in cold, arcane prose – in the published scientific papers that serve as the raw material for our report.

Necessary evil?

Some people argue that, though regrettable, such suffering is justified because significant health benefits accrue to people. The core of our report assesses the validity of that claim. Researched and written by a hospital doctor and a veterinary surgeon, the authors examine past and contemporary accounts of experimental procedures by the researchers themselves, as well as scientific reviews in leading specialist journals. They conclude that animal-based research into cancer, dementia, heart disease and Parkinson's has been a wasteful and futile quest – one that has failed to advance the cause of human medicine. We have identified 66 charities that use public donations to fund animal research (and nearly 80 that forswear the use of animals). We focus on Cancer Research UK, the British Heart Foundation, Parkinson's UK and the Alzheimer's Society because they are bodies of some standing and authority. Their collective annual income is currently more than £710 million, with Cancer Research UK taking £515 million of that total. At the other end of the scale is Parkinson's UK, which draws £17 million.

Policy of concealment

How much of their respective research budgets goes into funding animal experiments? We asked the charities directly but received, in response, rhetoric rather than detail. They would not say how many animals – and of which species – they use. Or how they are used. Through intense burrowing into specialist scientific libraries we did eventually find a good deal of information, and this forms the backbone of our report. But that material was more difficult to obtain

than it should have been. Occasionally, code numbers and phrases were favoured in place of straightforward terms such as 'non-human primate', or 'dog'. Deliberate obfuscation? We cannot know, but what is clear, is that the four charities concerned are loath to reveal to the general public details of the scale and nature of the animal research in which they are engaged. Animal Aid believes that transparency and accountability are vital. The public gives huge sums of money to these charities. In return, they should be told what they are paying for. They should have available to them details of the torments the animals experience, and also be offered verifiable information about the alleged fruits of such activities.

The immune-deficient 'mouse model'

As we have seen, the largest of the four charities is Cancer Research UK (CRUK). It currently spends more than £300 million on research (of all kinds; not just that which uses animals), even though it is widely recognised that cancer is largely preventable – lifestyle and environmental factors being responsible for more than 90 per cent of new cases. CRUK, however, continues to fund dozens of animal studies, mostly on mice, at academic and research institutions throughout the UK and overseas. Animal researchers have struggled for decades to mimic human cancer in mice. The 'triumph' of all this activity is strains of mice who have been stripped of their immune defences and into whom are introduced human cancer cells. Researchers often do no better than deposit this alien material (the 'xenograft') under the mouse's skin, thereby producing a 'subcutaneous xenograft'. The result is an unconvincing 'model' of the human condition. People with cancer generally have an active immune system that affects the way their cancer develops, whereas the mice are immune-deficient. And the introduced human tumour is deposited at a site from where, it is reported, it almost never spreads to other parts of the body – this spreading (metastasis) being the factor that decreases a patient's chances of survival.

A large percentage of the immune-deficient mice die in the womb or perish soon after birth from conditions that leave them unable to breathe or feed properly. Those who do survive face considerable challenges. Some develop (unplanned for) tumours and degenerative diseases. Others suffer anxiety – made evident through frenetic plucking of hair or whiskers from cagemates or from themselves. They are also susceptible to stress-induced circling, pacing, jumping or back-flipping.

Destroying the hearts of dogs and pigs

For heart disease research, healthy animals have often been grievously injured to produce a condition that is markedly different from those found in human patients. Dogs have had their hearts systematically destroyed over a period of months by the injection of polystyrene beads into their coronary arteries. With pigs, the favoured method is to place constricting rings around those same arteries. These narrow gradually over a period of weeks, resulting in a heart attack. The British Heart Foundation (annual income £213.7 million; expenditure on research £48 million) funds highly invasive experiments involving dogs, goats, pigs and rabbits. More recently, large numbers of fish have been the victims of their laboratory activities.

Many people will have seen the BHF's 'Mending Broken Hearts' advertising campaign, aimed at raising £50 million for heart failure research. It has featured talking zebrafish – a luckless minnow whose regenerative powers are claimed to offer hope for heart disease sufferers. Zebrafish have already been subjected to years of mutilating experiments. The BHF plans much more of the same. This report debunks the 'science' behind the BHF hype.

Forced to swim in a water maze

Equally unconvincing are the 'animal models' of Alzheimer's disease. Neurotoxins have been injected directly into the brains of rodents and monkeys, while rabbits have been poisoned with a diet of cholesterol and copper. The current fad is for genetically manipulated mice, some of whom are forced to swim around a pool of water from which they cannot escape or touch the bottom (mice are scared of being in water). Their task is to find a small platform on which they can rest. In later tests, the torment is increased when the platform is submerged.

A recent article in *Nature* magazine sums up where such activities have brought us. '…In recent years, and especially for neurodegenerative disease, mouse model results have seemed nearly useless.'*

Injecting poison into the brains of monkeys

Even more conspicuously vicious is the history of animal use for Parkinson's Disease research. In contrast to the positive steps achieved as a result of studying human Parkinson's sufferers, we show that animal research into PD has failed to deliver. Researchers, nonetheless, continue to 'model' the disease by injecting poison into the brains and circulation of primates and other animals.

For example, research funded by Parkinson's UK led on to a 2004 experiment in which 12 monkeys each suffered 18 separate brain injections 'in the hope of achieving longer-lasting behavioural deficits', with needles being left in their brains for two minutes after instillation of poison. Recipients of such treatment are likely to be left so severely disabled that they have to be hand-fed. They will suffer rigidity, poor coordination and loss of balance.

And highly toxic pesticides have been injected into the abdomens of mice, in order to kill or severely incapacitate them.

Valuable work

It is important to make clear that much of the educational and patient-support work carried out by the four charities under review does merit strong public backing. In the case of the Alzheimer's Society, more than 70 per cent of its nearly £60 million budget is devoted to 'care services', with 'just' £2 million spent on research. Substantially the largest share of Cancer Research UK's income, by contrast, goes on research (at the heart of which is a fixation on the 'mouse model'). What all four bodies have in common is a determination to conceal the nature and extent of the animal suffering for which they are responsible.

Research relevant to people

Our objective is to expose what is currently hidden, and thereby show an unsuspecting public just what their generosity is paying for. Beyond that, we want to press the four charities concerned (and others that fund animal experiments) to reappraise their research agendas. We wish to see them recognise that their animal research is as medically unproductive as it is cruel, and that they should be directing the funds bequeathed to them by the public into modern, non-animal research methods that are directly relevant to people.

* Schnabel, J. (2008). Neuroscience: Standard Model. *Nature* **454**, 682–685.

⇨ Extract from Animal Aid's publication *Victims of Charity, a report on the cruel and scientifically invalid experiments funded by medical research charities*, June 2011. Please visit www.animalaid.org.uk for further information.

Research scientist eh? Well, we have some interesting experiments to try on _you_ now!

In defence of animal experimentation

It's time that medical researchers were unequivocal in putting human need ahead of animal-welfare concerns.

By Patrick Hayes

How did a small, fairly insignificant group like Animal Aid manage to make a big splash this week on the alleged horrors of animal experimentation? Not because it is influential or powerful in its arguments, but because society feels queasy about vivisection. At a time when the authorities and even medical researchers seem unwilling to stand up and make an unequivocal case for the importance of animal experimentation, groups like Animal Aid are empowered to spread doubt and suspicion.

Animal Aid's campaign is a rehash of the same old anthropomorphic, misanthropic arguments: mice are being 'tortured in water mazes', zebrafish are being 'mutilated', pigs are being 'sacrificed' all for no real reason except seemingly to satisfy the perverse pleasure of sadistic medical researchers. The reasons given by Animal Aid for a financial boycott of four charities that benefit from animal experimentation – Cancer Research UK, the British Heart Foundation, Parkinson's UK and the Alzheimer's Society – are nothing the British public hasn't heard before.

Animal Aid's report *Victims of Charity*, which supposedly provides the evidence base that lends support to its advertising campaign, fails miserably in its attempt to suggest that animal 'suffering' should be prioritised over trying to find a cure for cancer or Alzheimer's. And the group's attempt to conclude that animal-based research is a 'wasteful and futile quest' that doesn't actually yield positive benefits to humans is laughable, contradicted by countless medical discoveries, from the use of dogs to extract insulin to treat diabetes to the experiments on armadillos that developed a cure for leprosy.

So why are major figures taking the Animal Aid campaign seriously, suggesting that a motley crew of bunny-worshipping nutjobs could have a major effect upon the public's financial support for medical research? Lord Willis of Knaresborough, chairman of the Association of Medical Research Charities, rightly dismisses the campaign as 'illogical and ill-conceived' but then suggests: 'It will have consequences for charities targeted as, during tight economic times, any small downturn in donations could really put back cures by decades.'

Why should even such a small downturn in donations happen? The assumption seems to be that the very presence of this advertising campaign will mean that – rather than seeing Animal Aid's arguments for the nonsense they are – financial supporters of these charities will somehow be fooled by these arguments and withdraw their financial support. Do they really think that a potential donor, initially inspired by trying to prevent others having to experience the suffering that a family member or friend went through, would suddenly have a change of heart in order to save a zebrafish?

Yet such concerns appear widespread. A report in the UK Independent asserts: 'Privately, the charities are concerned that the Animal Aid campaign could have an effect on donations – but they are also worried about tackling the organisation head-on in case it exacerbates the problem.'

When contacted by *spiked* yesterday, more often

it seemed that, privately, the charities were more concerned about giving publicity to a small bunch of hysterical no-marks than making the case for animal testing. All were willing to put forward statements about the importance of animal testing and engage in a debate, but they often came across as unnecessarily apologetic and defensive.

James Culling, head of individual giving, legacies and membership at Parkinson's UK, said that his charity was not concerned about the impact of the Animal Aid campaign on donations and that 'our members and supporters know that a small, but vital part of our research programme involves animals.'

Dr Kieran Breen, director of research and development at

Parkinson's UK, used the example of the Parkinson's drug Levodopa, 'which would not have been developed without the insights gained from research involving animals'. He argued that animal research would play a 'key role' in ultimately developing a cure for Parkinson's.

A strong case for animal testing was made by Dr David Scott, director of science funding at Cancer Research UK: 'Cancer survival has doubled over the last 40 years – that progress is based on the wide array of new treatments developed and tested using animal research.' Or, as a spokesperson for the British Heart Foundation argued, 'thousands of people are only alive today thanks to pioneering treatments such as pacemakers and heart transplants, which just wouldn't have been possible without involving animals'.

Such powerful defences of the importance of animal research are to be welcomed. However, all too often they are followed by an admission that such research is regrettable. Dr Scott, for example, emphasised: 'We do no research with monkeys, dogs or cats. We have strict ethical policies in relation to animals and follow rigorous government guidelines to ensure that animals are only used

where there's no alternative.' This was echoed by the British Heart Foundation, which stressed that animal testing is 'not a decision taken lightly but sometimes there is simply no alternative'.

While such clauses could be seen as an attempt to avoid appearing cold-hearted and unsympathetic to the suffering of animals, they actually reveal the extent to which concessions have been made to animal-rights protesters.

Nothing typifies the extent to which such concessions have been made more than the National Centre for the Replacement, Refinement and Reduction of Animal Research (NC3Rs), still flourishing under the UK Coalition Government and funded by a mixture of state and private money from a range of research organisations. The NC3Rs declares that the replacement of animals in testing 'is the ultimate aim for the centre, but as long as the use of animals continues to be necessary, every effort must be made to minimise the numbers used and improve their welfare'.

Such attempts to place restrictions on the types and numbers of animals experimented on is troubling, because it is having an impact upon research organisations throughout the UK. Yes, animal research may have saved the lives of millions from cancer, but could experimenting on dogs, cats and monkeys potentially save the lives of millions more? Such human-centred ethical considerations suggest that the objectives of major medical research organisations may have been worryingly compromised to satisfy small coteries of animal-rights protesters unable to differentiate between the value of self-conscious human life and that of an unreflective beast.

A number of the charities were quick to cite a recent opinion poll that showed 90 per cent of the UK public accept the idea of animal research to some degree, and three in five accept it unconditionally. Thanks, in part, to the strident

defence of animal research put forward by researchers like Tipu Aziz, Professor of Neurosurgery at Oxford, public opinion is currently stacked in favour of conducting animal experiments in order to save human lives.

However, this should not be taken for granted, and shying away from engaging in a public debate for fear that any such debate may lead to a shift in opinion is the worst thing that charities and researchers could do. Indeed, there is still considerable ground to be gained: the argument needs to be won with the other two out of five members of the public who don't yet accept animal research unconditionally. A strong case needs to be made for the abolition of the NC3Rs and the channelling of that research money instead into work that will benefit human lives. Moreover, there is much lobbying that should be done to scrap laws preventing experiments on great apes. All of these sops to the anthropomorphic fantasies of a minute anti-vivisection lobby are hindering the development of medical science.

Rather than being on the defensive when the issue of animal testing comes up in the public arena, medical researchers should instead be on the offensive, seizing the opportunity to defeat the feeble arguments of groups like Animal Aid and making a positive case for the vital importance of animal testing in transforming – and saving – the lives of millions of human beings. The abolition of existing 'ethical' restrictions on animal testing would remove barriers that are stifling medical progress and could be costing the lives of many more human beings.

22 June 2011

⇨ The above information is reprinted with kind permission from *spiked*. Please visit www.spiked-online.com for further information on this and other subjects.

Experiments where human cells are transplanted into animals should be better regulated, a report says

Channel 4 News looks into the debate of science versus 'Frankenstein's monster' fears.

A report from the Academy of Medical Sciences into the ethics of putting human material into animals for research purposes said more regulation is needed now, before possibilities that are explored in fiction start happening in reality.

While the report stressed that experiments at the more extreme end of the scale are not happening in the UK yet, its authors said they wanted to start the conversation now so that future decisions could be taken with the support of scientists and the public.

Many scientists believe that research of this type, where human genes are implanted into animals like mice and goats, has huge potential. It has already had some notable successes like the Down's mouse, a mouse implanted with the human chromosome linked to Down's Syndrome which has helped scientists understand more about the condition.

While the report found that the public is generally in favour of this research, it also looked at the point at which people have ethical issues with certain experiments. People are most concerned about research which involves the modification of the animal brain to create human-like 'cerebral' function – including creating animals which can speak – or fertilising human eggs or sperm in an animal.

The report said the Government should set up a national expert body and create different grades of experiment to provide guidance for scientists.

The 'Frankenstein fear'

The report said scientists needed to take seriously what could happen in the future, and consider 'the "Frankenstein fear" that the medical research which creates "humanised" animals is going to generate "monsters"'.

A member of the working group which produced the report, Dr Robin Lovell-Badge – who is a leading geneticist from the Medical Research Council's National Institute for Medical Research – told Channel 4 News: 'People are very odd. We all laugh when we see cartoons of talking meerkats or cats with opposable thumbs but they know they are not real. If we were actually doing that in the labs and they were made real, I don't think people would be so happy.'

He added: 'That's really why we did this report because we wanted to understand people's attitudes, and we recognise the concerns and that is why we're proposing this extra level of regulation at the point where people might start feeling revolted by the idea or uncomfortable. That is what is missing in regulation at the moment.'

Research where human material, including genes, is transplanted into animals is already used in many areas of medical research, such as in the battles to cure diseases like HIV and cancer. For example, scientists have implanted a human gene in goats which enables them to produce a human protein which is used to treat blood clotting disorders. They have also used mice with human liver cells to study diseases including HIV and hepatitis.

Dr Lovell-Badge said this kind of research was 'extremely important' and exciting for scientists because of the potential to help them understand disease as well as how genes work and the fundamental differences between human and animal behaviour.

Recommendations

But Professor Martin Bobrow, the chair of the working group, said experiments did need to be classified so that scientists breaking new ground were clearer over what was acceptable. He also said this kind of research should be supervised by a national expert body.

He said: 'The very great majority of experiments present no issues beyond the general use of animals in research and these should proceed under current regulation.

'A limited number of experiments should be permissible subject to scrutiny by the expert body we recommend; and a very limited range should not be undertaken, at least until the potential consequences are more fully understood.'

All animal testing in the UK is currently regulated by the Home Office, through the Animal Procedures Committee, and the Government said it would consider the report's recommendations.

⇨ A version of this article was first published by channel4.com/news and is reprinted with permission. Please visit www.channel4.com/news for further information on this and other subjects.

© Channel 4 2012

Key Facts

⇨ The Society for the Prevention of Cruelty to Animals (SPCA) was the world's first charity for the welfare and protection of animals, and was founded in a London coffee shop in 1824. Later, the charity received royal patronage from Queen Victoria and went on to become the Royal Society for the Prevention of Cruelty to Animals (RSPCA). (page 1)

⇨ In 2006 the Animal Welfare Act largely repealed and replaced the 1911 Protection of Animals Act. The Act also introduced a new offence of failing to ensure the welfare of an animal. Anyone found guilty of offences under the Act could be banned from owning animals, fined up to £20, 000 and/or given a prison sentence. (page 2)

⇨ The Red Tractor kitemark appears on billions of packs of meat, poultry and dairy products and is intended to reassure consumers that these products have been produced to the highest standards of animal welfare and environmental protection. (page 3)

⇨ It is illegal to sell an animal to any person whom you have reasonable cause to believe to be under 16. This includes transferring or agreeing to transfer ownership of an animal. (page 5)

⇨ Mortality rates at factory farms vary from one farm to another, but it is typical for around 5% of factory-farmed chickens to die before reaching slaughter weight. In a shed of 10,000 birds that means around 500 of them die or need to be culled before they even make it to six weeks of age. Chickens would naturally live for up to seven years or more. (page 7)

⇨ 31 million eggs are eaten in the UK each day. In the average 36cm tall 'battery cage' there are around 5 or 6 birds, and in the average 45 cm tall 'enriched cage' there are around 50 to 60 birds. (page 8)

⇨ The Jewish method of slaughter, Shechita, requires animals not to be stunned before slaughter. Islamic food rules for Halal meat can be satisfied with animals stunned before slaughter if they do not die as a result of the stun. (page16)

⇨ An estimated 40, 000 bulls are killed in Europe each year. The total number killed across the world is estimated at 250, 000. (page 17)

⇨ Recent opinion polls have shown that a significant majority of people are against bullfighting. 89% of British people would not visit a bullfight, whilst in Spain 67% are not interested in bullfighting. In France 69% of people oppose public funding for bullfighting. (page 17)

⇨ Worldwide, more than 40 million animals are killed for their fur – 85% are bred and killed on fur farms and the rest are trapped in the wild. The most commonly bred animals on fur farms are mink and fox, but it is also estimated that two million cats and dogs are also killed for their fur. (page 18)

⇨ There are around 6,500 fur farms in the EU. Europe is responsible for 70% of global mink fur production and 63% of fox fur production. The countries that farm the most animals for their fur are Denmark, China and Finland. (page 18)

⇨ Sealing is important to the people of coastal communities throughout the world. People in Australia, Canada, Estonia, Finland, Latvia, Lithuania, Greenland, Iceland, Namibia, Norway, Russia, Sweden, United Kingdom and the United States all hunt seals. (page 22)

⇨ Horse fighting occurs throughout the island of Mindanao in the southern Philippines during fiestas. Whilst it was outlawed in 1998 under the Animal Welfare Act, horse fighting organisers pay little heed to the law, and the events take place in broad daylight in public areas. (page 27)

⇨ 29 of the 34 animal species currently classified as Extinct in the Wild are actively bred in zoos, aquariums and other animal propagation facilities. (page 26)

⇨ In 2010, 3.72 million animals were used in scientific procedures in the UK. Most of the animals used are rodents and fish and cats, dogs and primates, such as macaques and marmosets, make up less than 0.5% of the animals used. (page 29)

⇨ Polls consistently show that around three-quarters of the UK public agree that animal research is necessary to advance medicine. (page 29)

Animal research

The process of using animals in scientific research. Also called 'animal experimentation' or 'animal testing'. Animal research for the purposes of testing cosmetic products is largely banned in the European Union. However, the use of animals in research and testing for medical purposes is still considered essential by the majority of the scientific community.

Animal rights

This term usually refers to the view that animals should be respected and treated in the same way as human beings. Animal rights campaigners reject the treatment of animals as property and campaign for their recognition as legal beings.

Animal stunning

Whilst stunning's purpose is to make an animal unconscious by electrocuting it, as opposed to killing it straight away, some methods of stunning may induce heart attacks. Head-only electrical stunning can induce unconsciousness without stopping the heart from beating, and this means that the animal is still alive when the throat is cut.

2006 / 2007 Animal Welfare Act

Passed in 2006 this animal welfare legislation came into force in 2007. Whilst it largely repealed and replaced the 1911 Protection of Animals Act, the law also made it an offence to fail to ensure the welfare of an animal, and to dock the whole, or any part, of a dog's tail. Anyone found guilty of committing offences could be banned from owning animals, fined up to £20, 000 and/or given a prison sentence.

Cetacean

A term which refers to large aquatic mammals who have hairless bodies, flippers and breathe through blowholes. Cetacean's resemble fish and include dolphins, whales and porpoises.

Factory farming

A method of farming where a large number of animals are confined within small spaces such as cages, crates and overcrowded sheds. The animals are specifically bred for the purpose of being 'factory farmed' and this means that they are breeds which are selected because they are fast growing or high producing.

Furrier

Furrier's are skilled craftsmen and women who use animal fur in order to produce fur garments.

Invertebrates

Invertebrates is a term which describes animals without a backbone, and is used to refer to insects, shellfish, octopuses, snails and other animals.

Propagation facilities

An environment where reproduction is encouraged. Endangered animals may be kept in propagation facilities in an attempt to increase their population.

Religious slaughter

The slaughter of animals according to religious rules or rituals. Examples of religious slaughter include Halal slaughter, an Islamic ritual, and Shechita, a Jewish tradition.

RSPCA

Originally known as the Society for the Prevention of Cruelty to Animals (SPCA), founded in 1824, the SPCA later became the Royal Society for the Prevention of Cruelty to Animals after receiving royal patronage by Queen Victoria. The charity work to rescue and rehabilitate thousands of animals each year, offer advice on caring for all animals and campaign for their protection.

Thalidomide

Introduced in the late 1950's thalidomide was a sedative drug given to pregnant women to help with morning sickness and aid sleep. However, the drug was withdrawn in 1961 after it was found to cause birth defects in some children whose mothers had taken the drug whilst they were pregnant.

Vegans

Vegans oppose the use of animal food products as well as material or bi-products which are produced by an animal. Vegans oppose eating meat as well as eating, or using, other animal products such as eggs and milk.

Assignments

The following tasks aim to help you think through the debate surrounding animal rights and provide a better understanding of the topic:

1. Look at the articles entitled 'If you really care about animals, please don't visit zoos' (page 24) and 'zoos and aquariums save the world's most endangered species' (page 26). Write a review of these articles, summarising the issues they raise and whether, in your opinion, zoos are a necessary part of animal protection and conservation.

2. Visit the RSPCA website and research the charity – how effective do you think this organisation is in protecting animals? What issues do the RSPCA consider the most challenging or find to be the most common? In your opinion how important is it that the public donate to charities such as the RSPCA?

3. Research animal rights organisations in your local area. Imagine that you work as a volunteer for one of these organisations and write eight blog entries talking about the work you do on a daily basis.

4. 'Animal research doesn't work and hasn't made any contribution to medical progress' (page 31). Do you agree with this statement? discuss in small groups and feedback to the rest of your class.

5. Design a storyboard for a Youtube video which explains the importance of global animal welfare and protection. The video should be interesting and engaging, providing a variety of information that summarises key animal welfare issues. At the end of the video you should also provide your audience with details of where they can go for further information.

6. Organise a class debate on the pros and cons of the fur trade using the articles entitled 'The fur trade' (page 18) and 'Fur: the natural responsible choice' (page 19) as inspiration. One half of your class will represent the fur trade's supporters and the other will represent the campaigners who want the fur trade to be abolished.

7. A recent poll has showed that '90 per cent of the UK's public accept the idea of animal research to some degree, and 3 in 5 accept it unconditionally' (page 38). Complete a survey of your friends, family and classmates to see if they agree with these statements. Write a report detailing your findings and how they compare to these statistics.

8. In small groups, choose either 'Questions and answers about factory farming' (page 7) or 'Myths and facts' about animal research (page 30) as starting points for a discussion. What are the main points raised in your chosen article? Do you consider animal welfare an important issue in today's society? Make notes on the discussion points raised in your group and feedback to the rest of your class.

9. Using television or the Internet, watch an episode of an animal-welfare based programme such as the BBC's 'Animal 24:7'. Write a bulleted list of the issues raised in the episode. What preventative methods do you think could have been taken to avoid some of the animal welfare cases? How crucial is it for a particular animal's health and safety that welfare officers intervene in certain situations?

10. Design a poster that summarises UK animal rights issues. Use 'Chapter One: animal rights in the UK' for information.

11. Imagine you are a local farmer. Write a letter to your local newspaper summarising the debate on animal farming and why you believe that ethical animal farming is important in the UK.

12. Design a PowerPoint presentation exploring the issues surrounding the use of animals and animal bi-products for food, medicine, entertainment and clothing. You should consider the benefits and disadvantages, as well as your own opinion.

13. Visit a news website, such as www.guardian.co.uk and research two recent stories that raise issues concerning the infringement of animal rights. Write a summary of the cases you have found and what action, if any, was taken to resolve them.

14. In groups of three, stage a radio interview discussing whether 'intelligent' animals such as whales and dolphins should be granted the same rights as humans. One of you should take the part of the radio host, asking questions, one should act in favour of animals being given human rights and one should argue against.

15. Imagine that you work for a charity that is campaigning to ban bullfighting. Create an information leaflet explaining facts and issues surrounding this form of entertainment.

Acknowledgments

LRC Radbrook

The publisher is grateful for permission to reproduce the following material.

While every care has been taken to trace and acknowledge copyright, the publisher tenders its apology for any accidental infringement or where copyright has proved untraceable. The publisher would be pleased to come to a suitable arrangement in any such case with the rightful owner.

Chapter One: Animal rights in the UK

What is animal welfare? © 2004–2012 SquareDigital Media Ltd, The Animal Welfare Act 2006, © RSPCA 2012, Questions and answers about factory farming, © Compassion in World Farming, We don't need mega-dairies, © Compassion in World Farming, Super farms are needed in UK, says leader of National Farmers Union, © Guardian News & Media Ltd 2012, An outrage in Belfast: the sad case of Lennox, the dog, © 2012 AOL (UK) Limited, Olympic opening plans branded 'wholly irresponsible', © Captive Animals' Protection Society, No ban on circus animals as Cameron acts as chief whip, © The Independent, Circuses to be banned from using performing wild animals, © Crown copyright, Religious slaughter, © Parliamentary copyright, What is done to stop halal slaughter?, © Compassion in World Farming.

Chapter Two: Global animal rights issues

What's wrong with bullfighting?, © 2011, League Against Cruel Sports, The fur trade, © Animal Aid 2012, Fur: the natural responsible choice, © British Fur Trade, Dolphins are 'people' say scientists, © belfasttelegraph.co.uk, PETA slavery case against SeaWorld dismissed, as whales are not people, © The9Billion, Seals and sealing, © International Fur Trade Federation, Why commercial sealing is cruel, © International Fund for Animal Welfare 2012, If you really care about animals, please don't visit zoos, © Merseyside Animal Rights, Zoos and aquariums save the world's most endangered species, © World Association of Zoos and Aquariums, Horse fighting, © 2012 Network for Animals.

Chapter Three: Animal research

Animal research: fast facts, © 2012 Understanding Animal Research, Myths and facts, © 2012 Understanding Animal Research, Ethical issues, © Nuffield Council on Bioethics 2012, Victims of charity..., © Animal Aid 2012, In defence of animal experimentation, © spiked 2000 – 2012, Experiments where human cells are transplanted into animals should be better regulated, a report says, © Channel 4 2012.

Illustrations:

Pages five and 36: Don Hatcher; pages 12 and 38: Angelo Madrid; pages 26 and 32: Simon Kneebone.

Images:

Cover, i and 24: © Steven Allan; page 3: © Griszka Niewiadomski; page 6: © Jackie Staines; page 8: © Dieter Hawlan; page 14: © Candie_N; page 17: © Steven Depolo; page 21: © Bill Davenport; page 23: © International Fund for Animal Welfare; page 27: © Gareth du Plessis; page 29: © 2012 Understanding Animal Research; page 38: © 2012 Understanding Animal Research.

Additional acknowledgements:

Editorial on behalf of Independence Educational Publishers by Cara Acred.

With thanks to the Independence team: Mary Chapman, Sandra Dennis, Christina Hughes, Jackie Staines, Jan Sunderland and Amy Watson.

Cara Acred

Cambridge

September, 2012